Jean-Jacques Rousseau

On the Social Contract

Second Edition

Jean-Jacques Rousseau

On the Social Contract

Second Edition

Translated by Donald A. Cress

Introduction and New Annotation by David Wootton

Hackett Publishing Company, Inc.
Indianapolis/Cambridge

Copyright © 2019 by Hackett Publishing Company, Inc.

22 21 20 19   1 2 3 4 5 6 7

For further information, please address
  Hackett Publishing Company, Inc.
  P.O. Box 44937
  Indianapolis, Indiana 46244-0937

  www.hackettpublishing.com

Cover design by Listenberger Design & Associates
Interior design by Elizabeth L. Wilson
Composition by Aptara, Inc.

Cataloging-in-Publication data can be accessed via the Library of Congress
Online Catalog.

ISBN-13: 978-1-62466-785-5 (pbk.)

The paper used in this publication meets the minimum requirements of
American National Standard for Information Sciences—Permanence of
Paper for Printed Library Materials, ANSI Z39.48–1984.

∞

Contents

Introduction

We are approaching the state of crisis and the century of revolutions.[1]

—The tutor in Rousseau's novel *Émile* (1762)

Citizen of Geneva[2]

Jean-Jacques Rousseau was by birth a citizen of Geneva.[3] His mother died as a consequence of giving birth to him, and his father was an unsuccessful watchmaker who fled Geneva when Jean-Jacques was ten to avoid prosecution for assault. Jean-Jacques became, in effect, an orphan. He briefly tried out as a pupil-clerk with a notary but was dismissed for stupidity. Just before he turned thirteen, he was apprenticed to an engraver. His master beat him; he responded by stealing, and his master beat him all the harder. When he was fifteen, Jean-Jacques went out of the city one Sunday on a jaunt. The city gates were closed a little early, and he and his friends found themselves locked out. Rather than return with his friends the next day for the inevitable beating, Jean-Jacques set out into the unknown. He was homeless, penniless, and friendless. He was to spend the rest of his life looking for a home, but he was incapable of finding one. Nothing could adequately correspond to his imaginary ideal, the home he would have had if his mother had lived.

Rousseau escaped from his immediate predicament by converting to Catholicism. Geneva, the city of John Calvin, was Protestant; converts were welcomed and protected by the authorities of the neighboring Catholic states. By converting, Jean-Jacques automatically forfeited his citizenship; he was no longer a citizen of Geneva. He was sent (on foot, 150 miles through the

---

1. Jean-Jacques Rousseau, *Émile, or On Education*, trans. Allan Bloom (New York: Basic Books, 1979), 194. *Émile*, as its subtitle indicates, is both a novel and a theoretical discourse.
2. I am grateful to John T. Scott for comments on a draft of this introduction.
3. On Rousseau and Geneva, see James Miller, *Rousseau: Dreamer of Democracy* (New Haven: Yale University Press, 1984); Helena Rosenblatt, *Rousseau and Geneva* (Cambridge: Cambridge University Press, 1997).

mountains) to Turin, where, after being instructed in his new faith, he found employment as a lackey—a menial servant wearing his employer's uniform. His first employer died, and when her possessions were being inventoried, it turned out a little silver ribbon was missing. Jean-Jacques had stolen it, but he accused an innocent serving girl. Both were dismissed, and for the rest of his life Rousseau was tormented by the thought that Marion, without a reference, faced a future of prostitution, destitution, and early death. Jean-Jacques was more fortunate: he found new employment and was soon being groomed for promotion. But the prospect of spending the rest of his life as a servant was intolerable to him and, after eighteen months in Turin, he set out back toward Geneva. Rousseau had experienced dependence, and for the rest of his life he clung desperately to independence. He had waited on the rich, and he had learned to hate them. Later he would write, "I hate the great; I hate their high status, their harshness, their pettiness, and all their vices, and I would hate them even more if I despised them less."[4]

Jean-Jacques returned, not to Geneva but to Annecy, thirty miles south of Geneva. There, when he first fled Geneva, he had been taken in by Françoise-Louise de Warens, herself a convert from Protestantism who was paid a pension to encourage others to convert. Mme de Warens, who was separated from her husband, was thirteen years older than Jean-Jacques, and he quickly fell in love with her. For a few years, he was unsettled: he spent a year wandering, spending time in Lausanne and Neuchâtel and pretending to be a music teacher, a job for which he was hopelessly ill equipped. He walked three hundred miles to Paris and briefly worked as a tutor. He walked back to be reunited with Mme de Warens, now in Chambéry, sixty miles south of Geneva. In 1732 Rousseau, now twenty, and Mme de Warens became lovers. Neither took much pleasure in their physical relationship. Rousseau preferred to pretend Mme de Warens was his mother, not his lover (he called her *maman*), and "felt as if I had committed incest,"[5] and Mme de Warens always insisted that she was incapable of erotic feelings (although she had lovers besides Rousseau). Rousseau, who had received no formal education, now had the run of an excellent library and little else but reading to occupy his time.

After six years, he found himself supplanted in Mme de Warens' affections, and two years later he left to become a tutor, first in Lyons, then in Paris. For eighteen months, he was secretary to the French ambassador

4. Letter to Malesherbes, January 28, 1762.
5. Jean-Jacques Rousseau, *The Confessions*, trans. J. M. Cohen (London: Penguin, 1953), 189.

to Venice but was dismissed for insolence. At the age of thirty-three, he returned to Paris, and there he tried to make a living writing music. He also became a research assistant to a wealthy couple, the Dupins. Louise-Marie-Madelaine was writing an endless feminist tract, and Claude was soon writing a vast, unreadable refutation of Montesquieu. Rousseau also fell in with Denis Diderot and Jean le Rond d'Alembert, who were embarking on an ambitious and subversive enterprise, the great *Encyclopédie*, a compendium of progressive thinking. Out of friendship, they commissioned him to write articles on music. Meanwhile he had taken up with Thérèse Levasseur, a laundress. She was not officially either his mistress or his wife (visitors mistook her for his housekeeper), but their relationship was to last until his death, and they were to have five children—each of whom was taken promptly to the Foundling Hospital and abandoned. This was not particularly uncommon (Rousseau himself noted statistics suggesting 25 percent of children born in Paris were abandoned),[6] but the death rate for infants handed in at the Foundling Hospital was very close to 100 percent. Rousseau long kept his abandoned children a secret, and when news of them spread it tarnished his reputation, which has never recovered.

In the summer of 1749, Rousseau was thirty-seven. He was living hand to mouth, with no security; he was one of five hundred or so writers (and perhaps a similar number of musicians) living in Paris, hoping to find some sort of success.[7] He had failed in career after career: a failed notary, engraver, tutor, music teacher, secretary, research assistant, composer. Rousseau was on his way (walking again) to visit Diderot, who was locked up in a prison outside Paris for having published a book, the *Letter on the Blind*, a defense of atheism. On his way, he paused to read an advertisement in a newspaper that announced a competition to write a short essay on the topic "Whether the restoration of the sciences and arts has contributed to purifying mores [or morals]." He later said that he was immediately overcome with a "dizziness like that of drunkenness."[8] "I beheld another universe and became another man."[9] He tells us that a whole system of ideas immediately

---

6. Jean-Jacques Rousseau, *Oeuvres complètes*, 5 vols. (Paris: Gallimard, 1959–1995), 3:528.
7. Robert Darnton, "Two Paths through the Social History of Ideas," in *The Darnton Debate: Books and Revolution in the Eighteenth Century*, ed. Haydn T. Mason (Oxford: Voltaire Foundation, 1998), 251–94, at p. 256; Darnton, *The Literary Underground of the Old Regime* (Cambridge, MA: Harvard University Press, 1982).
8. Letter to Malesherbes, January 12, 1762.
9. Rousseau, *Confessions*, 327.

became apparent to him—and close reading of the Discourse he proceeded to write suggests this is true. *The Discourse on the Sciences and the Arts*, which is an attack on progress, prosperity, and sophisticated civilization, not only won the prize; when published, it immediately made Rousseau famous—it was even promptly translated into English. Although in the next few years he wrote an opera and a play, he had now embarked on a career as an author, writing several defenses of the First Discourse.

In 1754 he wrote the Second Discourse, *On the Origin of Inequality*. Again, his target was contemporary French society. This time, before publication, he made a pilgrimage to Geneva, where he rejoined the Protestant church and became a citizen once again. Publication of the Second Discourse in 1755 was followed rapidly by publication of volume five of Diderot and d'Alembert's *Encyclopédie*, which included Rousseau's article on political economy or, rather we might say (for his subject is not economics but the administration of the state), on government. It was at this point that Rousseau adopted (or rather adapted) the idea of the "general will," which is at the heart of *On the Social Contract*.[10] The next year Rousseau left Paris to take up residence on the country estate of a friend, ten miles north of Paris, in a cottage named the Hermitage. From here he published in 1758 a *Letter to d'Alembert on the Theater*, which represented a sustained attack on the views held by Diderot, d'Alembert, and their associates—who had been, up to now, his good friends. The ostensible issue was whether Geneva was right to have a ban on theaters, and Rousseau was once again defending ancient virtue against modern sophistication.

The break with the leading figures of the French Enlightenment, which obliged Rousseau to leave the Hermitage, was crucial in helping him find his own voice. Three works followed in quick succession: *Julie, or the New Heloise* (1761), an epistolary novel about an affair between a young woman and her tutor (the title, only finalized in the third edition, is a reference to Heloise and Abelard, famous lovers of the twelfth century); *Émile, or On Education*, a fictional account of the education of a young man (May 22, 1762); and *On the Social Contract* (May 15, 1762). *Julie* and *Émile* were immediately enormously successful—*Julie* was the best-selling novel of the entire eighteenth century—and turned Rousseau into a "celebrity"; the word

---

10. There has been a great deal of work on the history of the idea of the general will, e.g., James Farr and David Lay Williams, eds., *The General Will: The Evolution of a Concept* (Cambridge: Cambridge University Press, 2015), but I take it that it was specifically a reading of Diderot's article on "Natural Right" in volume 5 of the *Encyclopédie* that shaped Rousseau's own thinking on the subject.

was new, and he uses it of himself.[11] People traveled long distances just to see him. His appearance in a public place caused crowds to gather.

One reason for Rousseau's celebrity is that all his readers understood that his books were, in some peculiar way, always about himself. To love the book was to love the man. They understood that in everything Rousseau wrote his subject was himself. The first word of his *Social Contract* is "I"; the last word is "me." Everything he wrote—and not just his *Confessions* or *Rousseau, Judge of Jean-Jacques*—comes directly out of a meditation on his own experience of life and is consequently about himself. Not entirely surprisingly, he was the author of a play, *Narcissus, or the Man Who Fell in Love with Himself* (1752). Who was Rousseau? When he writes about politics, he consistently describes himself as "Citizen of Geneva."[12]

According to Rousseau, the citizens of a state are always sovereign and cannot transfer their right to anybody else; in the making of laws they cannot be represented, and nobody can act in their name. Two things follow from this: first, laws are to be made by all the citizens together, which means (in Rousseau's world of slow communication), the citizens must all be physically gathered together in one place. Legitimate politics can take place only within a city-state. Geneva, a city-state, thus had the potential to be a legitimate political community; France did not.

As far as Rousseau was concerned, the large territorial states of his day were doubly illegitimate: first, they were too big; and second, they consisted not of citizens but of subjects. Their governments asserted that the members of the state had given up their original right to rule themselves and agreed that others should rule over them. In Rousseau's view such an agreement is simply impossible, and states claiming to be based on it are necessarily illegitimate. Thus the French state, governed by an absolute monarch, was illegitimate because it was despotic, but there was no way it could be reformed, because any large state must of necessity be illegitimate. One cannot derive from *On the Social Contract* a political program for reform or even revolution in France; but it was obvious to readers in Geneva that it represented a program for revolutionary reform in their own city.

It is easy for us to think that every sensible person is hostile, as Rousseau was, to despotism, but that is because our politics is the long-term product

11. See the 1781 foreword to the first Discourse ("What Is Celebrity?"). Also Antoine Lilti, "The Writing of Paranoia: Jean-Jacques Rousseau and the Paradoxes of Celebrity," *Representations* 103 (2008): 53–83.
12. "Citizen of Geneva," title pages of First and Second Discourses and *Social Contract*.

of the English Revolution of 1688 and of the American and French revolutions. In the mid-eighteenth century, the consensus was that some form of despotism represented the political future. David Hume, for example, argued that absolute government could be "civilized" and could represent the likely future for Britain.[13] The leading figures of the French Enlightenment declared their support for despotic rulers such as Frederick the Great of Prussia and Catherine the Great of Russia; their objection to French despotism was not that it was despotic but that it was unenlightened.

The term "enlightenment" comes from the German *Aufklärung*, and it is not one with which Rousseau was familiar. He often uses the adjective *éclairé*, which means literally "well lit" (an artist's studio should be *éclairé*) and was used metaphorically to mean "well educated." For Rousseau and his contemporaries, *éclairé* did not have the specific meaning of "enlightened." Rousseau knew that he was supposed to live in a *siècle des lumières*, "an age of lights," or an enlightened age. The term seems to have been invented by Pierre Bayle (1647–1706), who, more than anyone, was responsible for one central aspect of the Enlightenment, the attack on the truths of revealed religion.

Enlightenment philosophers did not agree on what ought to replace revealed religion. Some, like Baruch de Spinoza, Paul-Henri Thiry (Baron d'Holbach), and Denis Diderot, were atheists or pantheists; some, like Voltaire, were deists; and some, like Locke, wanted a more rational Christianity (Locke wrote *The Reasonableness of Christianity* [1695], and his disciple John Toland wrote *Christianity not Mysterious* [1696]), but, at a time when Protestants were being severely persecuted in France, all favored religious toleration and freedom of debate. A rejection of revealed religion and of a conventional Christian morality (of sexual continence, for example) was one of the first requirements if you were to think of yourself as a *philosophe*—the word means "philosopher," but it was used in France to refer to enlightened philosophers, public intellectuals rather than university professors.

The *philosophes* of the mid-eighteenth century were united by more than a rejection of revealed religion. They had rejected the certainties of

---

13. David Hume, "Whether the British Government Inclines More to Absolute Monarchy, or to a Republic" (1741), in *Essays, Moral, Political, and Literary*, ed. Eugene F. Miller (Indianapolis: Liberty Fund, 1987), 47–53. For his idea of a "civilized European monarchy," see his essays "Of Civil Liberty" (87–96) and "Of the Rise and Progress of the Arts and Sciences" (111–37). Note that, although Hume writes of "absolute monarchy," the word "absolutism" was introduced only in the nineteenth century; the eighteenth-century term for absolute rule (carefully avoided by Hume but used frequently by Rousseau) is "despotism."

both scholastic philosophy (still mainly taught in the universities) and of Cartesianism and had adopted the epistemology and psychology of Locke—a cautious empiricism, a willingness to recognize the intellectual coherence of materialism, and above all a belief that human beings are shaped by their environment and, hence, by their upbringing.[14] Thus, what united the *philosophes* was a conviction that society could be reformed—it could be made more equal, more tolerant, more skeptical.[15] What went with this was a belief in progress—scientific progress, technological progress, economic progress, philosophical progress. The second half of the seventeenth century had seen a debate over whether the "moderns" were the equal of the "ancients." The Enlightenment took it for granted that that debate had been settled in favor of the moderns: gunpowder and printing, the science of Newton, the philosophy of Locke, and the new commercial prosperity of the Dutch Republic and of England were irrefutable proof that the moderns had outstripped the ancients.

Rousseau lived in the middle of the age of Enlightenment; for a while, at least, he counted among his friends some of the greatest *philosophes*—Diderot, d'Alembert, and Hume. But he was never an Enlightenment philosopher. Although he was far from being an orthodox Christian, he was more sympathetic to Christianity than any proper *philosophe* should be. If he did not uphold a conventional Christian morality, he was all in favor of *virtue* (by which he meant old-fashioned pagan virtues, such as courage and frugality, not fashionable "virtues" like politeness and sociability, nor Christian virtues such as piety and chastity).[16] He believed strongly that we are shaped by our environment, but he did not believe in progress. In contrast to the leading figures of the Enlightenment, he was systematically hostile to despotism. Rousseau was thus *in* the Enlightenment, but he was not *of* the Enlightenment; indeed, he became one of the Enlightenment's leading critics, placing himself at the opposite pole from the Enlightenment's figurehead, Voltaire, on almost every subject.[17]

---

14. David Wootton, *Power, Pleasure, and Profit: Insatiable Appetites from Machiavelli to Madison* (Cambridge, MA: Belknap Press, 2018).

15. The classic text is Carl L. Becker, *The Heavenly City of the Eighteenth-Century Philosophers* (New Haven: Yale University Press, 1932).

16. "J'adore la Vertu": "Observations," in *Oeuvres complètes*, ed. Bernard Gagnebin and Marcel Raymond, 5 vols. (Paris: Gallimard, 1959–1995), 3:39.

17. See Mark Hulliung, *The Autocritique of Enlightenment: Rousseau and the Philosophes* (Cambridge, MA: Harvard University Press, 1998); Graeme Garrard, *Rousseau's Counter-Enlightenment* (Albany: SUNY Press, 2003).

Thus when Rousseau sat down to write *On the Social Contract*, he wrote as a citizen of Geneva who had broken with the Enlightenment consensus. Like every author, he needed a publisher, and his publisher needed to make a profit. The basic obstacle that authors and publishers trying to sell books in France faced was government censorship.[18] Diderot and d'Alembert were struggling to publish the *Encyclopédie* legally in France (they wanted the protection of a "privilege," a form of copyright, so that their publisher could recuperate his costs). They were faced with growing hostility from the authorities. In 1757, Robert Damiens had tried to assassinate Louis XV, and the attack on intellectual radicalism, which had been gathering momentum over the previous years, became intense.

Censorship was tightened significantly after Claude Adrien Helvétius' *On Mind* (1758), which had been approved for publication, was condemned to be burned by the Paris hangman. Most *philosophes*, however, chose to publish anonymously and abroad; this, for example, was how Voltaire's *Candide* appeared in 1759. Copies were then smuggled into France and sold under the counter, in exactly the same way as pornographic books. As a consequence, there was no copyright protection for author or publisher—successful works were quickly pirated—and it was almost impossible for an author, even the most successful, to live by writing. (Most successful authors relied on patronage of one sort or another, often in the form of a government pension. Voltaire was rich, but as a result of financial speculation, not royalties.)

Rousseau's approach to publication was different. After the first edition of the First Discourse (which appeared anonymously), he usually, as with *On the Social Contract*, published abroad but under his own name. His printer, Marc-Michel Rey in Amsterdam, would then seek permission to bring copies into France; in other words, Rousseau sought to avoid pre-publication censorship while still conforming to the law. The case of *Émile* was somewhat different. It was printed with official permission by Nicolas-Bonaventure Duchesne in Paris, although on its title page it claimed to have been printed by Jean Néaulme at The Hague in Holland—a book needed to look as if it had been banned if it was to sell well. Here too, then, Rousseau had sought to act within the law.

Rousseau hoped to operate within the law because he had recently acquired the support of powerful aristocrats, the duke of Luxembourg and the prince of Conti; and he had their support precisely because he had not

---

18. Robert Darnton, *The Forbidden Best-Sellers of Pre-Revolutionary France* (New York: Norton, 1995); Raymond Birn, *Royal Censorship of Books in Eighteenth-Century France* (Stanford: Stanford University Press, 2012).

signed up to the *philosophes'* program of progress and religious skepticism. In many respects he could be read as a reactionary rather than a progressive writer. This was true even of a key chapter in *Émile*, the profession of faith of the Savoyard vicar. As far as Rousseau and the *philosophes* were concerned, this was an attack on atheism—even if it could also be read as an attack on orthodox Christianity. Diderot wrote, "He has the religious on his side, and the interest they take in him is due to the bad things he says about the *philosophes*. Since they hate us a thousand times more than they love their God, they don't care that he has dragged their Christ in the mud, so long as he's not one of us."[19]

Diderot was wrong. On June 9, 1762, the book was banned by the *parlement* of Paris—the *parlement* being a court of law—and a warrant was issued for Rousseau's arrest. Given the support for Rousseau in the highest quarters, the matter was handled delicately. Duchesne was given time to hide his stock, and he continued to sell copies by the simple device of sticking a new title page on the front, so that he was no longer (ostensibly) selling the book that had been banned. Rousseau was warned that he was about to be arrested. The police passed him on the road but made no attempt to stop him.

Thus Rousseau had to flee France because his religious views—boldly published under his own name—were unacceptable. But a few days later, on June 19, both *Émile* and the *Social Contract* were burned in Geneva, the first because it was irreligious, the second because it was subversive. Read in Geneva, the *Social Contract* was subversive because it was an attack on the narrow oligarchy that controlled Genevan politics and an assertion of the rights of all citizens. It is important when reading the *Social Contract* to grasp that Rousseau intended it to be read as a commentary on Genevan politics but that when he wrote it he was living—and expected to continue living—in France. Rousseau was therefore cautious in what he said about monarchy (it is easy to see that his views imply a much more profound hostility to French absolutism than he explicitly states); he exhibited much less caution in his discussion of city-states.

After protests against the banning of his work in Geneva proved futile, Rousseau renounced his Genevan citizenship in 1763. The man who liked to sign himself "Citizen of Geneva" was no longer a citizen—indeed, he had only been one as an adult for nine short years, during which period he had spent only a few weeks in Geneva. Now, once again, he was homeless. He was not to publish another major work during his lifetime. Rousseau moved

---

19. Letter of July 18, 1762, quoted in Leo Damrosch, *Jean-Jacques Rousseau* (New York: Houghton Mifflin, 2005), 358.

Introduction

first to a village near Neuchâtel, Switzerland, but a religious mob drove him out and pressure exerted by the Genevan authorities prevented him from settling anywhere else in Switzerland. Eventually he was forced to take refuge in England. David Hume arranged for him to stay on a country estate in Wootton in Staffordshire. Here Rousseau had a paranoid breakdown—he became convinced that Hume was his enemy and was spying on him. Rousseau's fears were not entirely imaginary: Hume was indeed opening his letters and was trying to obtain a pension for him from the king of England (in Rousseau's eyes a pension represented dependence; he always insisted on earning his own living, and late in his life, when his income from publishing had disappeared, he lived by copying music). Rousseau fled England in disguise, moved around anxiously from one hiding place in France to another, living under an assumed name, and then, readopting his own name, settled once again in Paris in 1770. Evidently, he was once more receiving official protection, probably because he was playing a part in France's complex engagement in Polish politics.[20] In 1778 his health deteriorated (as a result of being run over by a large dog owned by an aristocrat), and he died in Ermenonville, outside Paris.

During his last years he had been writing a series of autobiographical works—*The Confessions*; *Rousseau, Judge of Jean-Jacques* (a text that is an extended expression of his paranoid delusions); and *The Reveries of the Solitary Walker* (all three published only after his death). When Rousseau died, he was famous as the author of *Émile* and *Julie*, and, though to a much lesser extent, as the author of the First and Second Discourses. The *Social Contract* had caused a stir in Geneva (where Rousseau had followed it up with a volume of *Letters Written from the Mountain* in 1764) but not elsewhere.

The Solitary Walker

How are we to understand Rousseau as a man and as an author? First, Rousseau was, from the moment he walked away from Geneva, a walker.[21] In *The Confessions*, he describes with delight the long walks of his youth, from Geneva to Turin and to Paris. But he also spent hours walking every

---

20. See Jean Fabre's introduction to the *Considérations sur le gouvernement de Pologne* in Rousseau, *Oeuvres complètes*, 3:ccxvi–ccxliii.
21. For insight into Rousseau's psychology, Ian Hacking, *Mad Travelers: Reflections on the Reality of Transient Mental Illness* (Charlottesville: University Press of Virginia, 1998) is helpful.

day (often searching for botanical specimens). It was while walking that he did his thinking (and daydreaming, for he constructed an elaborate imaginary world for himself), and his last, unfinished work was *The Reveries of the Solitary Walker*. Walking brought Rousseau close to nature, but it also allowed him to escape from society[22] and from the sense of belonging, of rootedness that goes with calling somewhere home. In Rousseau's view, the natural condition of human beings was to be solitary wanderers. Rousseau never owned a house of his own and was horrified when one critic assumed that he must have land of his own somewhere. He never settled anywhere.

So Rousseau was, by choice, an outsider—a condition he embraced when, at the age of fifteen, he turned away from the locked gates of Geneva. He called himself a citizen of Geneva, but he never lived there as an adult citizen. He did almost all his writing in France, where he constantly emphasized that he was not French. The epigraph of the First Discourse is a pair of lines from the Roman poet Ovid: "Here *I* [my emphasis] am the barbarian because they do not understand me." Ovid had been sent into political exile far from Rome (among the Sarmatians). Literally, a barbarian is someone who speaks incomprehensibly (he says "bababa"; the word is intended to be onomatopoeic). Ovid had no doubt that he was civilized and the Sarmatians were barbarians, but he realized that they saw the world rather differently. Rousseau's epigraph announces that what he has to say will seem outlandish to many—either he is seriously wrong or the established values of the day are topsy-turvy. Either way he is an outsider.

But Rousseau was at odds not just with the rest of the world; he was at odds with himself. He placed enormous emphasis on the responsibilities of parents for their children, but he abandoned his own. He admired antique manliness and insisted on the subordination of women (while Voltaire, for example, wrote in favor of female equality), but his dress seemed effeminate, he took to needlework, and his sexual preferences were masochistic. He attacked the theater but wrote plays. He said the French (unlike the Italians) were incapable of appreciating good music, but he tried to make a living as a composer in Paris. He praised Geneva but never lived there as an adult. He refused pensions from the kings of France and England, but he accepted the patronage of aristocrats (although he always insisted on paying rent). He submitted his books to the censor (in both France and Geneva), but he wrote books that he knew—or ought to have known—would be

---

22. "I was born with a natural love of solitude," letter to Malesherbes, January 4, 1762. See Tzvetan Todorov, *Frail Happiness: An Essay on Rousseau* (University Park: Pennsylvania State University Press, 2001), 31–53.

banned. He advocated a state religion but could not accept the religion of any state. He claimed that human beings are naturally good but that they are entirely responsible for their own corruption. He made a cult of honesty and integrity but presented himself in *The Confessions* as a liar and a thief. Rousseau did not think he was unfortunate to find himself constantly at odds with himself; his fundamental claim was that this has become an inevitable part of the human condition. Rousseau's work is one extended protest against this internal conflict.

Rousseau the outsider who always aspired to belong, Rousseau the man at odds with himself who always aspired to be undivided and at peace—it is these fundamental contradictions that left Rousseau no choice but to think in paradoxes.

Political Paradoxes

Rousseau's political theory is straightforward once one grasps the basic principles out of which it is constructed. His starting place is the paradox of the First Discourse: progress is a bad thing because it is morally corrupting. Human beings were better when their lives were simpler and less sophisticated. Underlying this argument—barely stated but already present—is a further paradox, the paradox of the Second Discourse: inequality is the root of all evil. Progress requires inequality because it requires some people to have the time to concentrate on literature, philosophy, or science. Free time is one of the luxuries that only come into existence with inequality, and all luxuries are corrupting. Wealth brings about moral corruption, and progress intensifies the process.

We live in societies founded on very different values. We believe—or at least most of us believe (although concern about climate change has led some to question these beliefs)—that progress, economic growth, and prosperity go hand in hand and are fine things. We believe that we should all be equal before the law but that inequalities of wealth are essential in a competitive, free-market economy—without them, there would be no progress, economic growth, and prosperity. It is natural for us to think that Rousseau is simply wrong.

Rousseau's contemporaries also thought he was wrong, but for them it was a little more complicated than it is for us.[23] They knew that a number

---

23. Christopher J. Berry, *The Idea of Luxury: A Conceptual and Historical Investigation* (Cambridge: Cambridge University Press, 1994).

of previous civilizations, particularly ancient Sparta and republican Rome, had been opposed to luxury, which they had associated with despotism and decadence, and that almost all previous societies thought that trade should be controlled and restricted (by guilds, for example).

Free trade, unrestrained economic growth, and the acquisition of luxuries by anyone with money to spare had not been defended before Bernard de Mandeville's *Fable of the Bees, or Private Vices, Public Benefits* (1714; translated into French in 1740).[24] Mandeville's claim was that a society of hardworking, prudent, parsimonious people would be poor, primitive, and easily conquered, while a society of spendthrifts, gamblers, drunkards, and pimps would be rich, civilized, and able to afford a powerful army. Rousseau and Mandeville were in fundamental agreement about the nature of contemporary society, but Mandeville approved of it and Rousseau was opposed to it. After Mandeville, in France, came Jean-François Melon, author of *A Political Essay on Trade* (1734), and Voltaire, who had defended luxury in a poem titled *Le Mondain* (The Man of the World, 1736). In attacking luxury, Rousseau could appeal to a long tradition of both moral and economic thinking, but he knew that his contemporaries were for the most part sympathetic—if not to Mandeville, who, like Rousseau, relished unpalatable paradoxes, then at least to Melon and Voltaire—and deeply hostile to traditional critiques of luxury, new wealth, and pleasure-seeking behavior.

In Rousseau's view the critique of progress and luxury—the claim that progress and prosperity are bad for you—opens the way to a more radical claim: human beings are born good but are responsible for all the evil in the world. The word "good" here is very slippery: Rousseau thinks human beings are born good simply because they are God's creation, and God made everything as it should be in the best of all possible worlds. But it is obvious that there is evil in the world, and it is clear that Rousseau does not believe in the orthodox Christian explanation for evil, the Fall, and Original Sin. Rousseau has a quite different explanation. According to him, natural men and women are, in a moral sense, neither good nor bad. They are concerned with their own survival; they are capable of feeling pity, but they have no capacity for moral thought or action.

Morality begins only with society, with language, with sustained interaction. Rousseau thinks of society and language as resulting from social evolution, assuming that the first human beings (like, or so he thinks, gorillas and orangutans) lacked both. Our own picture of human evolution is distinctly

---

24. On Mandeville, see E. J. Hundert, *The Enlightenment's Fable: Bernard Mandeville and the Discovery of Society* (Cambridge: Cambridge University Press, 1994).

different from Rousseau's conjectural history, but it is worth remembering that every child does begin without language, without a sense of belonging to a community, and without a moral code—language, society, and morality are indeed things that we have constructed for ourselves and that we are socialized into. (I realize that many people would insist that this is not true of morality. Rousseau, in this respect like every other Enlightenment philosopher, takes it for granted that we have no innate moral sense. Locke was held to have refuted the idea of an innate conscience. Consequently, we have to construct our moral principles on the basis of our experience.)

So in Rousseau's view we are all born amoral. Two things happen when we enter society: we acquire the capacity for vice, and we acquire the capacity for virtue. Rousseau's analysis of vice is clearer and more developed than his analysis of virtue, and this imbalance has caused a good deal of confusion. Vice is born of competition. Primitive men and women, wandering alone through the woods, think only of food, shelter, and sex. When these needs are satisfied, they have no further concerns. But social men and women are constantly comparing themselves to other people: which of us is the most attractive, successful, admired, and envied? All of these questions involve asking not how I feel about myself but how others think about me. Thus, social people begin to live outside themselves; what matters to them are the thoughts and feelings that others have about them. Because they have only limited access to these thoughts and feelings, they are forced to imagine what they must be. So they live in a largely imaginary world in which they lose touch with their own thoughts and feelings but become emotionally dependent on the thoughts and feelings they believe others are having about them. (One can readily see how someone who thinks this is how we live might end up having a paranoid breakdown, as Rousseau did.)

This competitive, alienated, imaginary world breeds vanity, which is for Rousseau the fundamental vice. His name for it is *amour propre* (self-love), which he distinguishes from *amour de soi* (love of self).[25] *Amour de soi* is a healthy instinct for self-preservation, neither moral nor immoral, but necessary; *amour propre* is (usually) a corrupt, competitive desire to seem better than others, to be envied. People suffering from *amour propre* do not merely

---

25. For discussions of Rousseau's understanding of *amour propre*, see N. J. H. Dent, "Rousseau on *Amour Propre*," *Proceedings of the Aristotelian Society: Supplementary Volumes* 72 (1998): 57–73; Frederick Neuhouser, *Rousseau's Theodicy of Self-Love* (Oxford: Oxford University Press, 2008); Niko Kolodny, "The Explanation of *Amour Propre*," *Philosophical Review* 119 (2010): 165–200; Anna Stilz, *Liberal Loyalty: Freedom, Obligation, and the State* (Princeton: Princeton University Press, 2009), 115–36.

have a car to get from A to B; they have a larger car than their neighbors, so that other people will see how important they are, or a faster car, so that others will see how vigorous they are, or a "classic" car, so that others will see what good taste they have. They identify themselves with objects (such as cars) and what they take to be the thoughts of others and lose any authentic sense of who they are. Consequently, even if they are successful—even if they are rich and admired—they are losers, dependent on others, incapable of authenticity. Rousseau's account of how we live in society depends on being able to distinguish between a *true* self and a *false* self, a *real* interest and an *imaginary* interest. I have a real interest in not being hungry or thirsty; I have an imaginary interest in acquiring a reputation as a gourmet cook or an expert on fine wines. Caught up in competition, we lose touch with our true selves and our real interests.

But something else happens (or can happen) when we enter society: we acquire the capacity to identify with the society as a whole. Suppose I live on a small island—let's call me an Islander. I decide that what would best improve the lives of my fellow Islanders would be a boat we could use for fishing, so I set about building a boat. Very likely, I hope that when I have finished my boat, people will be grateful to me and will admire me; we often compete to be thought more prudent or more virtuous than our neighbors. But in this case, I am not pursuing an imaginary good, but a real one; and I am not pursuing my own benefit, or not primarily my own benefit, but rather that of my community. It certainly helps that my interests and those of my fellow Islanders coincide—I would be unlikely to build a boat if I did not expect to eat some of the fish that would be caught. It certainly helps that I imagine that one day everyone will be grateful to me, but I work long hours because I know I am not just working for myself but for others. In other words, society makes it possible for me to be virtuous, provided I make an emotional commitment to the community to which that I belong.

It will be much easier for me to make this commitment if certain preconditions are met. It helps if my community is small enough for me to feel that I know everyone else in it—a community of strangers is a contradiction in terms. It helps if its members have a great deal in common and live similar lives; they will not be able to identify with each other if some are poor and some are rich, if some are powerful and some are weak, if some live by fishing and some live by hunting, or if they are divided by religion. We can summarize these preconditions as *proximity*, *equality*, and *similarity*. Rousseau's ideal community is a small town; the population of Geneva when Rousseau was growing up there was twenty thousand. Large, anonymous, unequal, diverse societies will foster vice, not virtue, because they will encourage competition, not a sense of solidarity. Rousseau thus offers a sociology of virtue. He also presents us with a profoundly uncomfortable conclusion: to achieve what we are truly capable of as human beings, we need to live in a society characterized by proximity, equality, and similarity; if we do not live in such a society then we will always be at odds with ourselves.

It is often said that Rousseau presents two alternative ideals: that of "man" (the individual) and that of "citizen" (the member of a community).[26] *Émile*, *Julie*, and *The Confessions* explore the idea of the good life as it can be constructed by one or two people within a larger, far from ideal, community. *On the Social Contract* explores the idea of the good life as it can be constructed within the political community of a small city-state (what the ancient Greeks called the "polis"; Rousseau repeatedly uses the word *politie*, which an educated person would have recognized as a French equivalent of polis but which was not a word to be found in contemporary dictionaries). Now it is perfectly true that Rousseau tries to tackle these two issues: how can I best live here and now (in eighteenth-century France) and how could I best live if I were fortunate enough to be an Islander? But Rousseau is always clear that true self-fulfillment depends on losing yourself in something bigger than yourself.

Aristotle said that human beings are by nature political animals, animals designed to live in a polis. Rousseau thinks that human beings are by nature solitary wanderers, but once they enter the world of society, they can achieve true fulfillment only within the polis. Outside the polis the best we can hope for is some sort of mitigated *amour propre*; inside the polis we can hope for virtue. Identifying with an *imagined* community (France or the United States) will not do, because it always leaves unanswered a fundamental question: Which is the real France?[27] The north or the south? Paris or the provinces? It is impossible to *be* French; you always have to be some particular sort of French person. It is even impossible to be a Parisian. If you live in Paris you cannot possibly know your fellow Parisians or feel for them (the population of Paris in Rousseau's day was more than half a million); but you can if you live in Paris, Texas (population in the 2010 census: 25,171). Rousseau is a small-town boy trying to make it in the big city while insisting that to succeed you have to betray everything you believe in.

---

26. Judith N. Shklar, *Men and Citizens: A Study of Rousseau's Social Theory* (Cambridge: Cambridge University Press, 1969).
27. Benedict Anderson, *Imagined Communities: Reflections on the Origin and Spread of Nationalism* (London: Verso, 1983).

We are now in a position to grasp the central paradox of Rousseau's political theory: that we can find freedom in obedience; indeed we can be forced to be free. Human beings are, Rousseau believes (following Locke), born free; in most political communities they are subjected to a form of dependence that amounts to slavery. We cannot go back to a presocial world, so how can we recover our freedom? This is the crucial puzzle that Rousseau believed he had solved in *On the Social Contract*. Rousseau's answer depends on a basic distinction between sovereignty and government—this is very close to the distinction between legislative and executive that would later become important for the U.S. Constitution. Sovereignty expresses itself through laws, and government expresses itself through decisions. The law says murder is a crime; the government prosecutes a particular individual for murder. The law says there shall be a national currency; the government decides that the face of George Washington shall appear on the dollar bill. The law says there shall be an army and a navy; the government appoints generals and admirals. The law gives the government the authority to impose speed limits; the government decides which particular roads will be limited to which particular speeds.

Sovereignty, Rousseau believes, should be exercised by the people (or at least all the adult males) as a whole. Let them gather at a town hall meeting and make decisions together. But when they think about what to do they must never ask themselves, "What would be good for me?" but only "What would be good for us?" In other words—Rousseau never puts it like this, but the thought is one he would have agreed with—they must vote as if from behind a veil of ignorance where they have no knowledge of their own particular circumstances and interests.[28] If they do this, their decisions will embody what Rousseau calls "the general will." Rousseau tells us that the general will is infallible, that it is always right. This seems very strange to us because we are used to thinking that the majority decisions of assemblies are often wrong. But in other contexts we are quite happy using concepts in which the ideal and the actual are inextricably confused: we believe that all laws are to be regarded as just, and once a jury has declared someone to be guilty or innocent we think it is nearly always wrong to second guess the jury's decision. Suppose the general assembly votes to ban cigarettes. I have spoken and voted against the ban because I think it will give rise to an illegal trade in cigarettes. But once the decision is made—once the general will is known—I must say to myself, "Now that we have a ban, I must help make sure it works." Far from adopting an oppositional mentality, I must

---

28. John Rawls, *A Theory of Justice* (Cambridge, MA: Belknap Press, 1971).

join in and identify with the majority. It is an indication of the novelty of Rousseau's argument that he has to invent a new word, *identification*, to explain his thinking.[29] Rousseau's argument may be new, but there is nothing psychologically odd about this "joining in" process. We do it all the time. When the coach picks a team we want the team to win, even if we do not agree with all the coach's choices. When a business decides on a future strategy, all the executives work to make it succeed, even if some of them previously advocated a quite different strategy. In the British political system, when the cabinet makes a decision its members are bound by "cabinet responsibility." They must defend, and accept joint responsibility for, a policy that some of them may have been actively opposing only a few hours before. All Rousseau requires of his citizens is that they engage in team thinking of this sort, and this will only be possible if they think of themselves as plain citizens, not as rich or poor, old or young, sailors, soldiers, or candlestick makers. If they vote on the basis of their individual interests, then the vote will simply establish which interest group is biggest; if they vote for what will benefit the community as a whole, then the vote ought to establish the general will.

But of course circumstances change and people make mistakes, which is why Rousseau insists that the community cannot be bound by its previous decisions. There can be no fundamental law, no constitution, because every law is a new and complete act of sovereignty. Moreover, since we are all born free, we can only become citizens by an act of choice: we must freely choose to give priority to our membership of a particular community. Then when we obey the general will we are living out our own free choice; even the minority, outvoted when a new law is enacted, obeys its own choice when it obeys the law.

It should now be apparent how human beings can be born free and be everywhere in chains: they are in chains whenever a will is imposed upon them that is at odds with the general will. It should also be apparent that people can be forced to be free. Suppose I decide to become an Islander, and we Islanders find ourselves at war with the Mainland. Then, as an Islander, I should be prepared to die for my community; while as an ordinary human being, of course, I would rather run away than fight. If I am conscripted I am being forced to be free, for no one can be free if we all put our particular interests ahead of our interests as a community. Rousseau is thus particularly

---

29. Pierre Force, *Self-Interest before Adam Smith* (Cambridge: Cambridge University Press, 2003), 24–34.

concerned to overcome the free rider problem.[30] I want other people to fight for my country, but I don't want to fight (and die) for it myself. I want other people to pay taxes, but I don't want to pay taxes myself. The solution is simple: I must be required to do what I want other people to do. It would be unfair to allow me to avoid paying the price (both in blood and money) for my freedom but to expect everyone else to pay.

It should also now be apparent that there is a fundamental ambiguity in Rousseau's theory of virtue. If I identify with the welfare of society as a whole and am prepared to put my own interests to one side, then I am virtuous. But in a society where everyone identifies with the whole, having team spirit is precisely what will be rewarded by the approval of others. In extended, unequal societies *amour propre* results in the vice of vanity; in tight-knit, egalitarian societies *amour propre* results in something indistinguishable from virtue. How could one recognize true virtue and distinguish it from benign *amour propre*? Only by finding it in someone who pursued the good of humanity in face of the opposition, rather than the admiration, of his fellow citizens—in Rousseau, for example.[31] But such cases will be rare exceptions that prove the rule that we are shaped by the communities in which we live.

It is striking that it is very difficult to give an account of Rousseau's political theory without employing terminology—for example, "imagined communities," "veils of ignorance," "free riders"—that was completely unknown to him. This terminology reflects late twentieth-century efforts to come to grips with paradoxical aspects of the relationship between individuals and communities, but Rousseau would be entitled to say that he had already thought these issues through.

Rousseau's Sources

Rousseau never received a day of formal education in his life. As a child he received his education from his relatives, and as a young man he was self-educated. But it would be a mistake to think that this means he was

---

30. Mancur Olson, Jr., *The Logic of Collective Action* (Cambridge, MA: Harvard University Press, 1965).

31. See, for example, Rousseau's self-description in "Préface d'une seconde lettre à Bordes," *Oeuvres complètes*, 3:103–5. But see also how Rousseau attributes even his own love of truth to the hidden working of *amour propre*: letter to Malesherbes, January 12, 1762.

in any way ill informed. Indeed not only is he exceptionally well informed, but he generally demonstrates excellent judgment; the texts Rousseau refers to when outlining his political theory are nearly all texts still read today (Machiavelli, Grotius, Hobbes, Pufendorf, Locke, and, of course, Montesquieu).[32] Rousseau did not consistently exercise such good judgment; he wrote at length on the political theory of the abbé of Saint-Pierre, who is now almost entirely forgotten. He did so partly to satisfy Mme Dupin, and writing about Saint-Pierre was an excuse for writing about a much less respectable figure, Hobbes.

Of all political theorists, Hobbes (the Hobbes of *De Cive*, for there is no evidence that Rousseau ever read *Leviathan*) is much the most important for understanding Rousseau, for Rousseau's political theory is fundamentally a reworking of Hobbes'. Rousseau thinks that Hobbes' intellectual system is "horrible," but Hobbes himself is "one of the finest geniuses who ever lived."[33] Hobbes argues that there is no law governing individuals in the state of nature and that they have a right to do anything to protect themselves. Rousseau agrees. Hobbes argues that a political community is constructed by all individuals coming together and agreeing that their own wills will conform to those of the sovereign. Rousseau agrees. Hobbes, though, thinks that the initial agreement is one in which every individual agrees that they will be represented by an individual (a king) or an assembly (a senate or parliament), whereas Rousseau argues that the individuals themselves form a corporate body, the sovereign, which can never be represented, although he does expect it to hand over much power to the government.

Where Hobbes believes that when a political community is founded a despotic power is necessarily established, Rousseau insists that the people (individually) must obey only themselves (collectively), thus they replace one sort of freedom by another: individual freedom is given up, but a free community is created. This community requires an executive (or, in Rousseau's terminology, a government), but this must be answerable to the people. Rousseau thus seeks to substitute a theory of direct democracy for Hobbes' claim that all legitimate authority is "despotical."

---

32. Locke is not mentioned by name in *On the Social Contract*, but he is frequently referred to in the Second Discourse.
33. For Rousseau's words ("horrible" and "one of the finest geniuses . . ."), see "The State of War" in Jean-Jacques Rousseau, *Basic Political Writings*, trans. D. Cress, ed. D. Wootton, 2nd ed. (Indianapolis: Hackett, 2011), 256. On Rousseau and Hobbes, Robin Douglass, *Rousseau and Hobbes: Nature, Free Will, and the Passions* (Oxford: Oxford University Press, 2015).

Rousseau's account of the place of religion in politics should also be seen as a reworking of Hobbes'. Hobbes thought that in all modern Christian societies political authority and religious authority were at odds and that the church must be made subordinate to the state. Rousseau agreed. Hobbes went further; he advocated a rigorous materialism, while Rousseau wanted to preserve a belief in God's beneficence and the soul's immortality, partly because he held that these beliefs encouraged virtue. And Rousseau, with a typical love of paradox, argued that religious intolerance is never justified—except as a response to intolerance.[34]

Where Hobbes and Rousseau fundamentally disagree is on war. Hobbes thinks that in the state of nature there is a war of all against all; Rousseau argues that human beings' interests start to conflict only when some individuals lay claim to so much property that there is not enough land for others, or the land that is left is not of as high a quality (an argument derived from Locke). The state, which should have been invented to further the interests of all, is (by a cunning sleight of hand) actually employed by property owners to protect their interests and disarm those without property. Thus war does not lead to the construction of the state; rather, the construction of the state leads to conflict between states (the conflict of all against all that Hobbes had read back into the state of nature), and it leads to conflict within the state (the exploitation of the poor by the powerful and the rich). As a consequence, we live in an unending state of war. Violence between states, and between rulers and subjects, may break out only occasionally, but the state is always preparing for violence. In Sparta, the ruling elite regularly declared war on its subservient underclass, the helots.

Rousseau thinks that an undeclared war of the rich against the poor takes place in every modern society. Carl von Clausewitz was later to say that war is the continuation of politics by other means; Rousseau's idea of a "state of war" implies rather that politics is the continuation of war by other means. Thus Hobbes is right: we need to find a way of escaping from a war in which we are all caught up, but we are only caught up in this war *because* we live in political communities. How, then, to escape? The abbot of Saint-Pierre had a utopian solution to this problem: the governments of Europe must get together and impose limits on each other (much as the United Nations seeks to use the collective force of all states to discipline some states). Rousseau thought it ridiculous to imagine that despotic governments would give

---

34. Rousseau hesitated over whether to mount a direct attack in the *Social Contract* on the religious intolerance of contemporary France and eventually decided not to. See Book IV, Chapter 8, note 48 (below, pp. 114–15).

up the quest for ever more power. How then could the small city-states he advocated defend themselves? Only by forming confederations. Rousseau is an early advocate of a federation of independent republics (perhaps the only respect in which he is a significant influence on the American Founding Fathers).

In addition to Mandeville (to whom Rousseau owes his account of the hypocrisy at the heart of commercial society), Hobbes (from a critique of whom he derives his account of popular sovereignty and of the state of war), and Locke (to whom he owes his account of the proper limits on private property in a state of nature), there is one other political theorist we need to have in mind when reading the *Social Contract*: Diderot. In volume five of the *Encyclopédie* (the volume in which Rousseau's article "Political Economy" appeared), Diderot published an article on *droit naturel* (natural right). There Diderot argued that in principle we have a moral obligation to the whole of humanity to do those things that humanity as a whole would want us to do. Thus, Diderot ultimately grounds our obligations toward other human beings in what he calls the "general will." Diderot's general will seems pretty pointless: it is infallible, but it is hard to know what it says, and if we disobey it nothing happens to us. It is this theory that Rousseau adopts and adapts in the *Social Contract*.

Rousseau localizes Diderot's universal general will; in place of the whole of humanity, he substitutes the members of a particular city-state. We can usually discover the general will, he thinks, through a democratic vote of all citizens. If we disobey the general will, we break the law and can be punished—and indeed, we can be forced to be free. Rousseau thus takes the idea of the general will and turns it from a moral concept into a political concept—and claims that this concept solves the problem of how we can belong to a political community while retaining our freedom.[35]

The City-State

There is of course a further source for Rousseau's political theory: the real constitutions of city-states. Rousseau made a careful study of ancient Greece and ancient Rome, of contemporary Venice (where he worked for

---

35. Patrick Riley, "Rousseau's General Will," in *The Cambridge Companion to Rousseau*, ed. Riley (Cambridge: Cambridge University Press, 2001), 124–53; Stilz, *Liberal Loyalty*, 57–84.

eighteen months), and of his own city of Geneva.[36] In Geneva there was a general assembly that embodied the community as a whole, but it had lost the power to meet unless it was summoned, and its agenda was controlled by the oligarchy. In Rousseau's eyes Geneva was a degenerate city-state, and if power could be wrested from the oligarchy and returned to the general assembly it might become once more a true republic. His own interventions in Genevan politics, particularly after the banning of the *Social Contract* and *Émile*, were designed to bring about this transformation.

Eighteenth-century Geneva was a bustling commercial city, producing luxury goods such as the exquisite, highly decorated watches for which it was famous. How could such a city once more become a true republic? Rousseau has what we might call a minimalist and a maximalist answer to this question. In order to understand the minimalist answer we need to look more closely at the structure of *On the Social Contract*. Book I deals with the social contract and rejects all despotisms. Book II deals with the general will and rejects all large states. It is in these books that Rousseau's radical, indeed revolutionary, arguments are to be found. Book III deals with government. Book IV is particularly concerned with voting in the Roman republic. These two books (until one gets to the discussion of religion, which is evidently an afterthought) contain Rousseau's more conservative arguments. Rousseau argues that his political principles are perfectly compatible with a wide range of different sorts of government, even monarchy. This argument depends on radically redefining the meaning of the word *government*: for Rousseau, the government is simply the executive and the judicial powers that administer and enforce the laws. Having thus redefined government it is easy for Rousseau to conclude that democracy (i.e., democratic government) is impractical: in practice specialist administrators are required, and it is essential to separate the enterprise of legislation (in which all must have a say and in which the general good must be the only object) and the activity of administration (which is best carried out by specialists who are concerned not with general principles but particular instances). But there is a sleight of hand involved in this argument, for Rousseau's legislature is the whole body of the people. And when Rousseau says that democratic government could only be practical in a small state, without luxuries, with considerable equality and simple morals, he is in fact describing the very conditions that must exist if the people are to be capable of identifying the common good or (which is the same thing) giving expression to the general will. By going

---

36. Sparta had a particular influence on Rousseau. See Elizabeth Rawson, *The Spartan Tradition in European Thought* (Oxford: Clarendon Press, 1969), 231–41.

on to discuss voting in classical Rome, Rousseau reinforces the (misleading) impression that his arguments are compatible with a large state, a numerous people, and a profoundly unequal social order.

It would seem correct, then, to turn around and say that, despite his disclaimers, Rousseau is a democrat, and he identifies himself as such in the preface to the Second Discourse, addressed to the republic of Geneva and written before he redefined the term "government." Two passages in *On the Social Contract* and one in the preface to the Second Discourse seem to give grounds for doubt as to whether Rousseau is really a democrat at all. In the preface to the Second Discourse he says that (as in Geneva) only magistrates should be able to propose new laws; in Book II, Chapter 3 of *On the Social Contract*, he says that there should be no communication between the citizens regarding prospective legislation; and he ends Book IV, Chapter 1 with these words:

> I could present here a number of reflections on the simple right to vote in every act of sovereignty, a right that nothing can take away from the citizens, and on the right to state an opinion, to offer proposals, to divide, to discuss, which the government always takes great care to allow only to its members. But this important subject would require a separate treatise, and I cannot say everything in this one.

It would thus seem possible to conclude that although Rousseau insists that all laws must be voted on by the people as a whole, this requirement is massively undercut by his willingness to see the government alone initiate all proposals for new legislation, and his insistence that the debate on new laws must take place only within the government. The result would be to give the citizens no more than a right of veto, and they would in effect play a purely passive role in the state.

But this simply cannot be Rousseau's intention, for he argues that the assembly of the people must be able to meet without being summoned by the government, and this would be pointless if they could not also control their agenda. And he frequently refers to the popular assembly as deliberating, which is scarcely compatible with the notion that only the government should deliberate and debate. Crucially, in letters 7 and 8 of his *Letters Written from the Mountain* (1764), a defense of *On the Social Contract*, he makes it clear that he wants power to lie with the popular assembly, not the executive. He acknowledges that it may be helpful to initiate some restrictions on the conduct of business in the popular assembly in order to ensure that it is orderly, and he clearly wants to prevent the emergence of organized parties; but he claims that this is a minor problem, relatively easy to resolve, and that the key concern must be to ensure that the government is answerable to the assembly. It is this second problem on which he concentrates his attention. Finally, of course, *On the Social Contract* is itself an example of a citizen stating an opinion; it would be odd indeed if its argument amounted to a condemnation of Rousseau's own behavior.[37]

How can one resolve this contradiction? The answer, I think, is that Rousseau saw in his own Geneva and in Venice striking examples of governments that had deprived the popular assembly of the right to initiate and debate legislation. As long as the popular assembly retained the right to vote, it was, in some limited sense, sovereign. But the fact that governments would always aspire to place limits on the assembly's right to state opinions, offer proposals, and divide and discuss does not mean that Rousseau thought that all such limits were proper and necessary. Some limits might be necessary to ensure the orderly conduct of business (although Rousseau noted that in England the House of Commons was subject to virtually no external controls), and the larger the popular assembly the more such restrictions might be necessary, but the main thrust of Rousseau's argument was to condemn the Genevan and Venetian constitutions as degenerate examples of popular sovereignty. Governments that claimed the right to speak on behalf of the people must necessarily be claiming the right to act as the people's representatives and thus be going beyond their legitimate authority and usurping the rights of the popular assembly.

It should thus be apparent that it might be possible to implement Rousseau's principles within a commercial city such as Geneva without bringing about an economic or cultural revolution. In that sense, Rousseau's proposals are intended to appear eminently practical. But would this be sufficient? A conservative reading of Rousseau is one that imagines creating a legitimate political order out of human beings as they actually exist, out of citizens who are vain, selfish, and competitive. If we turn back to Books I and II it should be apparent that this would not really be possible. If citizens are to identify the common good, they must identify with the general interest, not their particular interest.

How to transform ordinary watchmakers, notaries, and engravers into citizens? This, Rousseau tells us, is the role of the legislator, whose concern is not simply with the establishment of a sound constitution, but with the transformation of the character and values of the members of the community. His task is not just the construction of a constitutional machine, but

---

37. John T. Scott, "Rousseau's Anti-Agenda-Setting Agenda and Contemporary Democratic Theory," *American Political Science Review* 99 (2005): 137–44.

also the transformation of human nature. This requires something more than mere reasoning and voting: people must be compelled without force, and persuaded without being convinced. The only means of achieving this is through religion, and it is striking that in a note Rousseau praises John Calvin, who had exercised political as well as religious authority in Geneva. It would require a Calvin to bring about the economic, cultural, and moral transformation required to turn ordinary town dwellers into true citizens.[38]

Much discussion of the general will fails to place it in the context of this required transformation of human nature. "Rousseau scholars disagree," writes David Lay Williams, "on whether his constructive political theory is fundamentally formal or substantive," that is to say, on whether Rousseau is primarily concerned with a set of procedures (every citizen must have a vote) or a set of outcomes (the law must be concerned with the general good).[39] Rousseau is certainly concerned with both procedures and outcomes, but it is important to remember that the general will is a *will*. Citizens will only will the common good if they cease to be corrupted by *amour propre*, if they identify with the community. Procedures alone will be insufficient in the absence of a profound commitment to something greater than self-interest.

In Rousseau's view moral action, indeed free action, only becomes possible when people concern themselves with the common good, not their own good. To be concerned with your own private interests is to be enslaved by what you think others think of you, to become captivated by your own imagination. To act justly, to think morally, to be free requires an escape from the narrow boundaries of the self, an embrace of the community. The general will is thus an expression of a sense of community, and not simply a sum of individual wills. Rousseau's constructive political theory is not just formal and substantive; it also entails a psychology of identification and a sociology of incorporation.

Thus *On the Social Contract* falls into two halves. The social contract, the general will, and the legislator of Books I and II point to a radically egalitarian society, one which rejects wealth and luxury (as Calvin's Geneva rejected dancing, playing cards, and theaters)—a society of Islanders in which the preconditions of proximity, equality, and similarity are met. But Books III

---

38. John T. Scott, "Rousseau and the Melodious Language of Freedom," *Journal of Politics* 59 (1997): 803–29.

39. David Lay Williams, *Rousseau's Social Contract: An Introduction* (Cambridge: Cambridge University Press, 2014), 251.

and IV suggest that, in the absence of a legislator capable of transforming human nature, there is still much that can be done to bring the government under the control of the citizens.

The French Revolution

In the years immediately before the French Revolution, everyone was reading Rousseau (particularly the newly published *Confessions*), but no one was reading the *Social Contract*. In 1910 Daniel Mornet surveyed the catalogues of five hundred French private libraries for the years 1750–1780. He found 185 copies of *Julie* and one solitary copy of the *Social Contract*. A hundred years of further research has done nothing to alter the picture Mornet drew.[40] So if Rousseau was a cause of the French Revolution, it was not through his political theory; it was through his fundamental claim that human beings are naturally good and that consequently there is no excuse for injustice—a claim readers would have encountered in *Julie* and *Émile* rather than in the *Social Contract*.

Almost overnight, the French Revolution changed everything. Between 1789 and 1799 there were thirty-two editions of the *Social Contract* in French—eight in 1792 alone.[41] When people were looking for a philosopher who advocated political revolution, they turned at once to Rousseau—partly because he was widely believed to have been the inspiration behind a democratic uprising that had taken place in Geneva in 1782.[42] One man above all constantly called on Rousseau as the guiding spirit of the revolution: the leader of the Jacobins, Maximilien Robespierre. He found in Rousseau much that served his purposes—a belief in the goodness of human nature, a love of virtue, a hatred of inequality, and the outline of a civil religion.

The question of Rousseau's significance for the French Revolution is so central to any understanding of the revolution that it cannot be answered without committing oneself to a theory of what the revolution was really all about. Much recent literature has taken Rousseau as the emblem of a new type of language, a language that constantly rejected moderation; for this literature, the revolution is to be understood as a series of speeches. On this view, Rousseau shaped the rhetoric of revolutionary extremism. An older literature

---

40. Miller, *Rousseau: Dreamer of Democracy*, 134; Darnton, *Forbidden Best-Sellers*, xvii–xviii, 67.
41. Miller, *Rousseau: Dreamer of Democracy*, 143.
42. Ibid., 140–42.

argued that the revolution stumbled from crisis to crisis, and Rousseau became the philosopher of the revolution as it was driven, almost accidentally, to more and more radical expedients.[43] Neither approach seems to me to capture the central feature of the role of Rousseau's books in the revolution.

On May 31, 1793, an armed insurrection of the sansculottes brought Robespierre and his allies to power. Their power base was the Jacobin Club, which sought to control the National Assembly by claiming to speak for the people, to be an organ of direct democracy; its power depended on its ability to take control of the streets of Paris. This power lasted less than a year, for Robespierre himself was taking power away from the Jacobins and the sansculottes by the time of his own fall. He was executed on July 28, 1794. This brief year was the heyday of Rousseauism during the revolution, and the reason for this is very simple: Rousseau had rejected the principle of representation in favor of the principle of direct democracy, and he had accepted the logic of this position by turning back in his mind to the city-states of the ancient world.

Fundamentally, the French Revolution was not French: the revolution took place in Paris, and Paris claimed the right to determine the fate of France. The sansculottes and the Jacobins claimed to speak for Paris and for France and thereby claimed the right to control the National Assembly of representatives. They backed up their claim with armed force. Rousseau was the only theorist who could be made to speak for a revolution that took place in the streets and squares of a single city. What mattered about Rousseau, then, was that he was a theorist of *civic* politics, of urban politics, not national politics.

Here the contrast with the American Revolution is crystal clear. The American Revolution stretched across thirteen colonies; no one city had a dominant position, which is why the government eventually had to be located in a brand-new city, Washington, D.C. From its beginning, the American Revolution was rooted, inevitably, in the principle of representation. Radicals like Paine wanted democratic, unicameral representative assemblies with unlimited powers; the Founding Fathers wanted the separation of powers, bicameralism, and an entrenched constitution. But nobody questioned the underlying principle of representation; and nobody in America took Rousseau's *Social Contract* seriously.

So the place of Rousseau in the French Revolution comes down to the relationship between Paris and the Provinces:[44] Rousseau, as an advocate

---

43. Darnton, "Diffusion vs. Discourse," in *Forbidden Best-Sellers*, 169–80.
44. Richard Cobb, *Paris and Its Provinces, 1792–1802* (Oxford: Oxford University Press, 1975).

of direct democracy, provided a spurious justification for the idea that the course of the revolution should be decided on the streets of the capital city. I say a spurious justification because if Robespierre exploited one key feature of Rousseau's political philosophy, he also misrepresented him utterly. Rousseau had made clear that the people—all the people—must choose. The revolution substituted Paris for the nation, the sansculottes for Paris, the Jacobin Club for the National Assembly, the Committee of Safety for the executive, terror for justice. Rousseau had never intended to justify substitutions of this sort, substitutions that made possible the concentration of absolute power in the hands of a few, and the sacrifice of the lives of vast numbers of innocent individuals to a revolutionary government claiming to act on behalf of a people whose wishes it had no intention of respecting. Rousseau had done his utmost to insist both on the rights of *all*, not of some faction or mob, and on the rights of *each*—the right of each individual to a fair trial according to the law.

In short, Rousseau would have been horrified by the revolution and he would have loathed Robespierre. He saw civil conflict in Geneva in 1737; he called it a "hideous spectacle." He saw a father and son preparing to fight on opposite sides. He resolved, he would later say, "never to take part in any civil war, and never to uphold freedom by arms."[45] When conflict broke out again in Geneva in 1765, in large part provoked by Rousseau's own publications, Rousseau hastily detached himself from the radical cause and called for restraint. Rousseau provided ammunition for revolutionaries, but he had no stomach for revolution.

Rousseau was incapable of seeing into the future. He writes often about "revolutions," but even he could not imagine the American and French revolutions. When Rousseau writes of revolutions, he has in mind the major political upheavals described by René-Aubert de Vertot (1655–1735) in his books on the "revolutions" of ancient Rome and of modern Sweden and Portugal—civil wars and coups d'état we would call them, rather than revolutions. Rousseau has been accused of being the author of a totalitarian political theory, but of course Rousseau could never imagine Nazi Germany or Stalinist Russia; he *was* familiar with what he called *despots*, a term that covered ancient Roman emperors such as Caligula, contemporary Ottoman rulers, the contemporary ruler of France, Louis XV, and, above all, his predecessor Louis XIV. It seems paradoxical indeed to accuse someone who hated despotism, who described himself as having an "indomitable spirit of

---

45. Miller, *Rousseau: Dreamer of Democracy*, 20, 126.

liberty," of seeking to establish totalitarianism.[46] This does not, of course, absolve him of all responsibility. Above all, by consistently giving priority to the community over the individual, the general will over the wishes of individuals, Rousseau invited misinterpretation and misrepresentation. But we can hardly blame him for failing to foresee events without parallel in previous history.

Shortly after the fall of Robespierre, a report to the National Convention recommending that Rousseau's remains be transferred to the Panthéon captured well the complex and ambiguous relationship between Rousseau's political theory and the revolution:

> *The Social Contract* seems to have been made to be read in the presence of the human species assembled in order to learn what it has been and what it has lost.... But the great maxims developed in *The Social Contract*, as evident and simple as they seem to us today, then [on first publication] produced little effect; people did not understand them enough to profit from them, or to fear them, they were too much beyond the reach of common minds, even of those who were or were believed to be superior to the vulgar mind; in a way, it is the Revolution that has explained to us *The Social Contract*.[47]

Of course we can go on reading the *Social Contract* as the handbook for political revolution, but when we do so we are not reading the book that Rousseau intended to write; we are reading Robespierre's *Social Contract*, not Rousseau's.

Rousseau's French

What is a good translation? One view is that the text should read so well that one can almost forget that one is reading a translation: Rousseau should be turned into a writer of twenty-first–century English. Another view is that, as far as possible, the language and sentence structure of the original should be retained: we should be constantly reminded that we are reading a text written in a different language in a different era. Translations of classic texts are of necessity always something of a compromise between these two approaches.

---

46. Letter to Malesherbes, January 4, 1762. The classic text, much debated, is J. L. Talmon, *The Origins of Totalitarian Democracy* (London: Secker and Warburg, 1952).
47. Quoted in Miller, *Rousseau: Dreamer of Democracy*, 163.

No translation, however brilliant, can give us information that is essential for the understanding of any classic text. In the first place, a good translation will often avoid what seems to be the obvious equivalent English word for reasons that at first seem puzzling. For example, *industrieux* does not mean "industrious" in eighteenth-century French; it means "skillful," as "industrious" did in Shakespeare's English. It only comes to mean "industrious" in nineteenth-century French. It would therefore be simply misleading to translate *industrieux* as "industrious." Sometimes words in French are ambiguous, so that their English equivalent is unclear. Thus, eighteenth-century French has no word for "parental," so *paternel* sometimes means gender-specific "paternal" and sometimes gender-neutral "parental" (just as the masculine pronoun sometimes refers only to males and sometimes to any human being).

Where translations inevitably fall short is in failing to alert us when words are new (Rousseau's words "identification" and "perfectibility," for example) or being used in a new sense (Rousseau gives new meanings to the words "city," "sovereign," and "government"),[48] and they give us no sense of which words are simply missing from the language (Rousseau complains at one point that he might appear to contradict himself, but this is only because he lacks the right words to convey his meaning).[49] In Russian, for example, there are no definite or indefinite articles (no words for "the" or "a"), yet every translation from Russian inevitably conveys the impression that there are, and obscures the choices the translator has had to make. Every reader of Rousseau needs to know that "social" was an unfamiliar word when he used it in the title of the *Social Contract*.[50] Three years later Diderot wrote the article "Social" for the *Encyclopédie*, which begins, "SOCIAL, adj. (Gramm.) a word recently introduced into the language." We talk about social contract theories, but we do so only because Rousseau put the word "social" in the title of his book; neither Hobbes nor Locke writes of a "social contract." Rousseau was in the forefront of a movement to isolate what he called (in words that seem straightforward to us) the "social system."[51]

---

48. On "city," Rousseau was presumably following Diderot's article for the *Encyclopédie*, vol. 3 (1753).
49. See *Social Contract*, Book II, Chapter 4, note 6 (below, p. 23).
50. John Lough, "The *Encyclopédie* and the *Contrat social*," in *Reappraisals of Rousseau*, ed. Simon Harvey et al. (Manchester: Manchester University Press, 1980), 64–74.
51. *Social Contract*, Book I, Chapter 9 (below, p. 18). Letter to Malesherbes, January 12, 1762.

We have already seen another example of Rousseau's innovative use of language: Rousseau uses the word *politie*, and the obvious translation is "polity," but no translation is going to tell you that the word is unusual in the French of Rousseau's day, so unusual that Rousseau wrote to his publisher warning him not to let the copyeditors correct it to *politique*.[52] He needs the word because he has no word for a city-state; he makes do with the word *cité* (city), which he redefines as a community of citizens rather than an urban conglomeration.

This example brings us to the very heart of Rousseau's political theory. *Politie* and *cité* are nouns. For Rousseau the equivalent adjective is *civil*, as in *société civile* and *religion civile*. The standard English translations are "civil society" and "civil religion." These are terms commonly used in English, and so these are the translations one should prefer. But *société civile* is the French translation of the Latin *societas civilis*, and the standard English translation for this in modern English would be "civic society." In eighteenth-century French there is no word for "civic," and *civil* conveys a range of meanings from "urban" to "civilized." When Rousseau writes of *société civile*, we have to decide whether he means urban society, civilized society, or (its root meaning) a society characterized by having citizens (a self-governing society, a civic society). Certainly he never defines "civil society" as being something different from the political community, as we would. So, too, when he writes of *religion civile* we have to remember that *civil* for Rousseau refers back to the city-states of ancient Greece and Italy; the civil religion is, in the first place, the religion of a polis. We say the United States has a civil society and a civil religion. Rousseau would have found this usage puzzling, as the United States is not a polis. In his view there can be no "civil society," and perhaps no "civil religion," in a nation-state.

How we understand *politie* and *civil* is thus central to how we understand Rousseau's political theory. Central to his moral theory is another problematic term: *amour propre*—commonly translated as "vanity," but vanity is always a vice, and as we have seen, *amour propre* can sometimes be virtuous. "Vanity" is a good translation if it reminds us that *amour propre* had standardly been a vice in writers prior to Rousseau, a bad translation if it makes us think it is always a vice in Rousseau's own writing and thus obscures the way in which his argument differs from that of his predecessors. Another key term is *moeurs*, which means "customs," "habits," or "ways," and, more broadly, everything that a modern anthropologist might include within the

---

52. Letter to Rey, December 23, 1761.

term "culture."[53] *Moeurs* has an English equivalent in "mores," but it also bears on our understanding of Rousseau's words *moral* (adjective) and *morale* (noun). It is easy to regard these as straightforwardly equivalent to "moral" and "morality," but in the French of Rousseau's day *moral* and *morale* refer to *moeurs* in general as well as to morality in particular. The words "culture" and "civilization" do not yet exist in the French of Rousseau's day; Rousseau's equivalent terms are *moeurs* and *morale*.

So when Rousseau answers the question posed by the Academy of Dijon, "Si le rétablissement des sciences et des arts a contribué à épurer les *moeurs*" (Whether the restoration of the sciences and the arts contributed to the purification of mores), *moeurs* can mean "morals," "culture," or both. Equally problematic are the apparently simple words "sciences" and "arts." In the French of Rousseau's day a *science* is any system of knowledge (including philosophy, even theology), and an *art* is any skilled activity, including metallurgy and shipbuilding as well as poetry and painting. Broadly speaking, Rousseau's *sciences* are theoretical, and his *arts* are practical, and between them they include knowledge in all its many forms. As for "restoration," the implicit reference is to the restoration (or rebirth) of knowledge that we call the Renaissance. Since the Renaissance is above all about the restoration of classical learning, Rousseau's answer is doubly paradoxical. He argues that progress is bad for us and that the recovery of classical learning in particular may make us apparently civilized, but it prevents us from being citizens. We have civility but we do not have civic virtue; we have culture but we do not have morality; we have politics but we do not have citizenship. Rousseau's whole argument depends on distinctions that we would express by contrasting "civil" and "civic," "culture" and "morality," and "politics" and "citizenship."

The problem of translation is not just that Rousseau's words and our words do not match up in any simple correspondence, for we can run into difficulties even when they do. Take the word *peuple*, a word that occurs over and over again in *On the Social Contract*. There's an obvious and straightforward English translation: "people." But in French the word *peuple* is followed by a singular verb, while in English it is followed by a plural verb. Thus the first sentence of the American Constitution begins "We the People." The subject of the verbs that follow ("do ordain and establish") is both "We" and "the People"; this is unproblematic because both take a plural verb. But Rousseau writes *le peuple est assemblé*, the people is assembled,

---

53. "I argue that Rousseau invented anthropology," says Darnton in "Two Paths through the Social History of Ideas," 273.

not "the people are assembled." Does this make it easier for him to think of the people as having a common identity, a single will? We use singular verbs for "family," "community," and "nation," but if "We the People" is always plural, then perhaps as a consequence our political thinking is of necessity more individualist and less collectivist than Rousseau's.

Is it possible to sum up in a sentence or two the difference between the language available to Rousseau for discussing politics and society and our language? It is. The rise of the social sciences has meant that our language provides a whole range of ways of distinguishing empirical from normative arguments. Rousseau's vocabulary—terms like "moral" and "civil"—encourages a constant slippage back and forth between the two. Even "social," which we normally use to provide descriptions of how things *are* rather than how they *should be*, is defined by Diderot in a way that elides the normative and the descriptive: "a word recently introduced into the language to designate the qualities which make a man useful in society, well-equipped to engage with other men: the *social* virtues."[54] David Hume had defined what we call "the fact-value distinction" or "the is-ought problem" in his *Treatise of Human Nature* (1739), but this book, as Hume put it in "My Own Life," "fell dead-born from the press."[55] Rousseau would never have encountered "the fact-value distinction."

Rousseau does not distinguish, as we would, between normative and empirical arguments, not because he is writing in French but because he is writing in the eighteenth century. He would have had equal difficulty making the distinction in eighteenth-century English, and when Hume did make the distinction it was scarcely noticed (or understood) by his contemporaries. However, by attacking the conventional values of his age, by exposing what he called "the contradictions of the social system,"[56] by using "nature" as a normative concept to criticize society, Rousseau made it peculiarly difficult for everyone else to carry on taking their own value system for granted. If a whole range of distinctions—between morality and culture, principle and practice, values and facts—have come to seem obvious distinctions to us, that is a measure of the extent to which Rousseau's way of thinking provoked an intellectual crisis, a crisis that has profoundly shaped our modern culture.

54. Quoted in Lough, "*Encyclopédie* and the *Contrat social*," 70.
55. Hume, *Essays*, xxxi–xli, at xxxiv.
56. Letter to Malesherbes, January 12, 1762.

Suggestions for Further Reading

The classic edition of Rousseau's political writings is Jean-Jacques Rousseau, *The Political Writings*, ed. C. E. Vaughan (Cambridge: Cambridge University Press, 1915)—now out of copyright and so available on the Internet. The standard modern edition is volume 3 of the Pléiade edition of Rousseau's *Oeuvres complètes* (Paris: Gallimard, 1964).

The major sources for Rousseau's biography are the letters to Malesherbes of 1762 (which have been repeatedly translated into English) and the posthumous *Confessions*. An excellent modern biography is Leo Damrosch, *Jean-Jacques Rousseau: Restless Genius* (Boston: Houghton Mifflin, 2005). The classic study of Rousseau is Jean Starobinski, *Jean-Jacques Rousseau: Transparency and Obstruction* (1957; English translation, Chicago: University of Chicago Press, 1988). A valuable introduction is provided by Patrick Riley, ed., *The Cambridge Companion to Rousseau* (Cambridge: Cambridge University Press, 2001), and a brief survey is found in Tzvetan Todorov, *Frail Happiness: An Essay on Rousseau* (University Park: Pennsylvania State University Press, 2001).

The two classic texts on Rousseau's political theory are Ernst Cassirer, *The Question of Jean-Jacques Rousseau* (1932; English translation, New York: Columbia University Press, 1954) and Judith N. Shklar, *Men and Citizens: A Study of Rousseau's Social Theory* (Cambridge: Cambridge University Press, 1969). Admirable are James Miller, *Rousseau: Dreamer of Democracy* (New Haven: Yale University Press, 1984) and Arthur M. Melzer, *The Natural Goodness of Man: On the System of Rousseau's Thought* (Chicago: Chicago University Press, 1990). For a recent account of Rousseau's political thought by an English-language political philosopher, there is Joshua Cohen, *Rousseau: A Free Community of Equals* (Oxford: Oxford University Press, 2010). The argument of *On the Social Contract* is analyzed in David Lay Williams, *Rousseau's Social Contract: An Introduction* (Cambridge: Cambridge University Press, 2014). On gender and politics, see Joel Schwartz, *The Sexual Politics of Jean-Jacques Rousseau* (Chicago: University of Chicago Press, 1984) and Lynda Lange, ed., *Feminist Interpretations of Jean-Jacques Rousseau* (University Park: Pennsylvania State University Press, 2002). Good starting points for thinking about two of Rousseau's key concepts are Patrick Riley,

"Rousseau's General Will," in *The Cambridge Companion to Rousseau*, ed. Riley (which should be supplemented by a reading of Diderot's essay "Droit naturel," translated in Diderot, *Political Writings*, ed. John Hope Mason and Robert Wokler [Cambridge: Cambridge University Press, 1992]) and N. J. H. Dent, "Rousseau on *Amour Propre*," *Proceedings of the Aristotelian Society: Supplementary Volumes* 72 (1998): 57–73.

Chronology

1642	Hobbes publishes *De Cive*
1671–1678	Pierre Nicole's *Essais de morale* offers a crucial account of how self-interest and *amour propre* can lead to a semblance of virtuous behavior
1689	Locke publishes *Two Treatises of Government*
1695	Bayle begins publication of his *Historical and Critical Dictionary*
1712	Rousseau is born in Geneva June 28; mother, Suzanne, dies July 7
1714	Mandeville publishes *The Fable of the Bees*
1722	Rousseau's father, Isaac, flees Geneva to avoid arrest; Rousseau boards with a brother and sister, Jean-Jacques and Gabrielle Lambercier
1725	Rousseau is apprenticed to an engraver, Abel Ducommun
1728	Rousseau runs away from Geneva, meets Mme de Warens, goes to Turin, and formally converts to Catholicism
1729	Rousseau moves in with Mme de Warens in Annecy
1730	Rousseau tries to become a music teacher in Lausanne and Neuchâtel
1731	Rousseau visits Paris, returns to Mme de Warens, now in Chambéry, and tries out as clerk in a land survey office
1734	Voltaire publishes *Letters Concerning the English Nation*
1735	Rousseau moves to Les Charmettes, a country house rented by Mme de Warens
1737	Rousseau visits Montpellier
1738	Rousseau is supplanted in Mme de Warens' affections by Jean-Samuel-Rodolphe Wintzenried
1740	Rousseau becomes tutor to the sons of M. de Mably in Lyons
1742	Rousseau moves to Paris, aspiring to write music
1743	Rousseau becomes secretary to the French ambassador in Venice

1744	Rousseau leaves Venice, returns to Paris, and becomes friends with Diderot
1745	Rousseau meets Thérèse Levasseur, who will bear him five children, all abandoned
1746	Rousseau is employed as secretary and researcher by Mme Dupin
1747	Rousseau's father dies
1748	Montesquieu publishes *The Spirit of the Laws*
1749	Rousseau conceives the argument of the First Discourse (*Discourse on the Sciences and the Arts*) on the road to Vincennes
1750	The First Discourse wins the Academy of Dijon's prize and appears in print
1751	First volume of Diderot and d'Alembert's *Encyclopédie* is published
1754	Rousseau visits Geneva and converts back to Protestantism
1755	Publication of the Second Discourse, *Discourse on the Origin and Foundations of Inequality among Men*, and of the third, *Discourse on Political Economy*
1756	Rousseau and Levasseur move to The Hermitage
1757	Rousseau breaks with Diderot and other leading *philosophes*
1758	Rousseau moves to Montmorency; publishes *Letter to d'Alembert on the Theater*, completing his break with the leading figures of the French Enlightenment; Helvétius publishes *De l'esprit*, which is promptly condemned
1759	Rousseau becomes friends with the duke and duchess of Luxembourg; Voltaire publishes *Candide*; the *Encyclopédie* is officially suppressed
1761	Rousseau publishes *Julie, or the New Héloïse*
1762	Rousseau publishes the *Social Contract* and *Émile*; both are condemned in Paris and Geneva; he flees France and settles near Neuchâtel, Switzerland
1763	Rousseau renounces his Genevan citizenship
1764	Rousseau publishes an attack on the Genevan authorities, *Letters Written from the Mountain*; Voltaire reveals the secret of Rousseau's abandoned children

1765	Rousseau is driven from Neuchâtel and finds temporary refuge on the Île de Saint-Pierre; last volume of Diderot and d'Alembert's *Encyclopédie* is published
1766	Rousseau moves to England (to Wootton in Staffordshire) and begins writing *The Confessions*
1767	Rousseau flees to France, living here and there under an assumed name, protected by the prince of Conti
1768	Rousseau goes through a form of marriage (which is not legally valid) with Levasseur
1770	Rousseau resumes his real name and moves to Paris
1771	Rousseau gives readings from *The Confessions* but is ordered by the authorities to stop
1772	Rousseau begins work on *Rousseau, Judge of Jean-Jacques*
1776	Rousseau begins work on *The Reveries of the Solitary Walker*, is knocked over in the street by a huge dog and never fully recovers
1778	Rousseau moves to Ermenonville, outside Paris, where he dies July 2
1780	*Rousseau, Judge of Jean-Jacques* is published
1782	First half of *The Confessions* is published; democratic uprising in Geneva
1789	Second half of *The Confessions* is published; the French Revolution begins
1793	Execution of King Louis XVI (January 21)
1794	Execution of Robespierre, followed by the transfer of Rousseau's remains to the Panthéon in Paris
1801	Death of Thérèse Levasseur

Translator's Note

The translation, which is based on the excellent *Oeuvres complètes de Jean-Jacques Rousseau*, vol. 3 (Paris: Pléiade, 1964), is adapted with slight modifications from Jean-Jacques Rousseau, *The Basic Political Writings*, 2nd ed. (Hackett, 2011). Square brackets [ ] enclose editorial annotations, most of which were provided by David Wootton.

D.A.C.

Rousseau described his Social Contract *as an extract from a larger work,* Political Institutions, *which he had begun in 1751 (and the idea of which, he says, dated back to his time in Venice, 1743–1744).*[1] *An incomplete first draft ("the Geneva manuscript") exists and was first published in 1887. This, in all likelihood, is a surviving remnant of the draft Rousseau sent to his publisher, Marc-Michel Rey, on December 23, 1760. On August 9, 1761, Rousseau declared that his book was finished and ready to be published. In 1758 Rousseau was still working on his* Political Institutions, *and it seems likely that* On the Social Contract *took on its present form only after he abandoned that undertaking, although in the published texts Rousseau occasionally repeats entire passages from the* Discourse on Political Economy *of 1755. In any event, a crucial source for his argument was Diderot's article "Natural Right," published in November 1755. The argument of the* Social Contract *can only have taken on its final form after Rousseau read this article (presumably only shortly prior to its publication in the* Encyclopédie*). Conceived in 1743, begun in 1751, rethought in 1755, reconstructed in 1758, and largely completed by the end of 1760, the* Social Contract *was published alongside* Émile. *Rousseau was even afraid that in France it would be thought of as an appendix to his treatise on education.*[2] *But the two books were intended to have different audiences:* Émile *was to be published in France for a French audience; the* Social Contract *was to be published in Holland and, Rousseau said, "was certainly not intended for the French."*[3] *Rey received the manuscript on December 4, 1761 and had copies on sale by the middle of April 1762. In the space of a few months, he printed five thousand copies in two editions—the first an octavo and the second a duodecimo, which appeared a month after the first. These were swiftly followed by pirated editions. But in France the book was banned immediately upon being submitted for approval. There was no prospect of its being approved, it was made clear, even if revised. Pirated copies were soon being smuggled in, but they found few readers. In Geneva, however, the book was widely distributed in the fortnight before it was banned. Rousseau claimed in 1764 that "everybody" had a copy. The book had found its intended audience; its banning provoked a crisis in Geneva, while it passed virtually unremarked in France.*

D.W.

---

1. [Letter to Moultou, January 18, 1762.]
2. [Letter to Duchesne, May 23, 1762.]
3. ["Ce livre n'étant point fait pour la France," letter to Duchesne, May 23, 1762.]

ON THE

SOCIAL CONTRACT,

OR

PRINCIPLES

OF

POLITICAL RIGHT

By J.-J. Rousseau,

Citizen of Geneva

Let us propose fair terms for the peace settlement.

—*Aeneid*, XI[1]

---

1. [Rousseau gives the Latin: "foederis aequas / Dicamus leges" (*Aeneid*, bk. 11, line 302).]

FOREWORD

This little treatise is part of a longer work I undertook some time ago without taking stock of my abilities, and have long since abandoned. Of the various selections that could have been drawn from what had been completed, this is the most considerable, and, it appears to me, the one least unworthy of being offered to the public. The rest no longer exists.

BOOK I

I want to inquire whether there can be some legitimate and sure rule of administration in the civil order,[2] taking men as they are and laws as they might be. I will always try in this inquiry to bring together what right permits with what interest prescribes, so that justice and utility do not find themselves at odds with one another.

I begin without demonstrating the importance of my subject. It will be asked if I am a prince or a legislator that I should be writing about politics. I answer that I am neither, and that is why I write about politics. Were I a prince or a legislator, I would not waste my time saying what ought to be done. I would do it or keep quiet.

Since I was born a citizen of a free state and a member of the sovereign,[3] the right to vote is enough to impose upon me the duty to instruct myself in public affairs, however little influence my voice may have in them. Happy am I, for every time I meditate on governments, I always find new reasons in my inquiries for loving that of my country.

---

2. [Rousseau has only one word, *civil*, where we have two, "civil" and "civic." This translation generally translates *civil* as "civil," but it should be remembered that "civic" may also be right.]

3. [The free state is the Republic of Geneva; Rousseau held that the sovereign authority in Geneva was the general council, an assembly of all the citizens.]

Chapter 1

Subject of the First Book

Man is born free, and everywhere he is in chains. He who believes himself the master of others does not escape being more of a slave than they. How did this change take place? I do not know. What can render it legitimate? I believe I can answer this question.

Were I to consider only force and the effect that flows from it, I would say that as long as a people are constrained to obey and do obey, they do well. As soon as they can shake off the yoke and do shake it off, they do even better. For by recovering their liberty by means of the same right that stole it, either the people are justified in getting it back or else those who took it away were not justified in their actions. But the social order is a sacred right that serves as a foundation for all other rights. Nevertheless, this right does not come from nature. It is therefore founded upon agreement.[4] The real question is: what is this agreement? Before coming to that, I ought to substantiate what I just claimed.

Chapter 2

Of the First Societies

The most ancient of all societies, and the only natural one, is that of the family. Even so, children remain bound to their father only as long as they need him to take care of them. As soon as the need ceases, the natural bond is dissolved. Once the children are freed from the obedience they owed the father and their father is freed from the care he owed his children, all return equally to independence. If they continue to remain united, this no longer

---

4. [Rousseau uses three words with related meanings: *contrat* (contract), *pacte* (compact), and *convention* (agreement). In Rousseau's day *convention* means "agreement" (*accord* or *pacte*); it does not mean the same thing as modern English "convention"— Oxford English Dictionary (OED), senses 9 and 10: "a rule or practice based upon general consent," in other words, a tacit rather than an explicit agreement; it acquired this meaning in French only in the nineteenth century.]

takes place naturally but voluntarily, and the family itself is maintained only by means of agreement.[5]

This common liberty is one consequence of the nature of man. Its first law is to see to his preservation; its first concerns are those he owes himself; and, as soon as he reaches the age of reason, since he alone is the judge of the proper means of taking care of himself, he thereby becomes his own master.

The family therefore is, so to speak, the prototype of political societies; the leader is the image of the father, the people are the image of the children, and, since all are born equal and free, none give up their liberty except for their utility. The entire difference consists in the fact that in the family the love of the father for his children repays him for the care he takes for them, while in the state, where the leader does not have love for his peoples, the pleasure of commanding takes the place of this feeling.

Grotius denies that all human authority is established for the benefit of the governed, citing slavery as an example.[6] His characteristic method of reasoning is always to present fact as a proof of right.[7] A more logical method could be used, but not one more favorable to tyrants.

According to Grotius, it is therefore doubtful whether the human race belongs to a hundred men, or whether these hundred men belong to the human race. And throughout his book he appears to lean toward the former view. This is Hobbes' position as well. On this account, the human race is divided into herds of cattle, each one having its own leader who guards it in order to devour it.

Just as a herdsman possesses a nature superior to that of his herd, the herdsmen of men, who are their leaders, also have a nature superior to that of their peoples. According to Philo,[8] the emperor Caligula reasoned thus, concluding quite properly from this analogy that kings were gods, or that the peoples were beasts.

Caligula's reasoning coincides with that of Hobbes and Grotius. Aristotle, before these three, had also said that men are by no means equal by nature, but that some are born for slavery and others for domination.[9]

---

5. [Here Rousseau follows Locke, *Two Treatises of Government*, Second Treatise, ch. 5.]

6. [Hugo Grotius, *On the Law of War and Peace*, bk. 1, ch. 3, §8.]

7. "Learned research on public right is often nothing more than the history of ancient abuses, and taking a lot of trouble to study them too closely gets one nowhere." *Treatise on the Interests of France along with Her Neighbors*, by the Marquis d'Argenson. This is just what Grotius has done.

8. [Philo of Alexandria (20 BC–AD 50), *Embassy to Gaius* XI (76).]

9. [Aristotle, *Politics*, bk. 1, chs.1-2 (1252a/b).]

Aristotle was right, but he took the effect for the cause. Every man born in slavery is born for slavery; nothing is more certain. In their chains, slaves lose everything, even the desire to escape. They love their servitude the way the companions of Ulysses loved being turned into beasts.[10] If there are slaves by nature, it is because there have been slaves contrary to nature. Force has produced the first slaves; their cowardice has perpetuated them.

I have said nothing about King Adam or Emperor Noah, father of three great monarchs who partitioned the universe, as did the children of Saturn, whom some have believed they recognize in them.[11] I hope I will be appreciated for this moderation, for since I am a direct descendant of one of these princes, and perhaps of the eldest branch, how am I to know whether, after the verification of titles, I might not find myself the legitimate king of the human species? Be that as it may, we cannot deny that Adam was the sovereign of the world, just as Robinson Crusoe was sovereign of his island, as long as he was its sole inhabitant. And the advantage this empire had was that the monarch, securely on his throne, had no rebellions, wars, or conspirators to fear.

Chapter 3

On the Right of the Strongest

The strongest is never strong enough to be master all the time, unless he transforms force into right and obedience into duty—hence the right of the strongest, a right that seems like something intended ironically and is actually presented as a basic principle.[12] But will no one explain this word [strongest] to me? Force is a physical power; I fail to see what morality can

---

10. See a short treatise of Plutarch titled "That Animals Reason." [*Moralia* XII.67. Ulysses' companions were turned into beasts by Circe.]

11. [Rousseau is referring to the central claim of *Patriarcha*, by Robert Filmer, published posthumously in 1680 and refuted by John Locke, Algernon Sidney, and James Tyrrell, that all rulers take their authority from Adam via Noah. The claim that Saturn in Greek mythology is the equivalent of Noah in the Old Testament is to be found, for example, in Urbain Chevreau, *Histoire du monde*, 2 vols. (Paris, 1686, vol. 2, 243).]

12. [Rousseau's target here is Hobbes.]

result from its effects. To give in to force is an act of necessity, not of will. At most, it is an act of prudence. In what sense could it be a duty?

Let us suppose for a moment that there is such a thing as this alleged right. I maintain that all that results from it is an inexplicable mishmash. For once force produces right, the effect changes places with the cause. Every force that is superior to the first succeeds to its right. As soon as one can disobey with impunity, one can do so legitimately; and since the strongest is always right, the only thing to do is to make oneself the strongest. But what kind of right is it that perishes when the force on which it is based ceases? If one must obey because of force, one need not do so out of duty; and if one is no longer forced to obey, one is no longer obliged. Clearly then, this word "right" adds nothing to force. It is utterly meaningless here.

Obey the powers that be. If that means giving in to force, the precept is sound, but superfluous. I reply it will never be violated. All power comes from God[13]—I admit it—but so does every disease. Does this mean that calling in a physician is prohibited? If a brigand takes me by surprise at the edge of a wooded area, is it not only the case that I must surrender my purse, but even that I am in good conscience bound to surrender it, if I were able to withhold it? After all, the pistol he holds is also a power.

Let us then agree that force does not bring about right and that one is obliged to obey only legitimate powers. Thus my original question keeps returning.

Chapter 4

On Slavery

Since no man has a natural authority over his fellow man, and since force does not give rise to any right, agreements alone therefore remain as the basis of all legitimate authority among men.

If, says Grotius, a private individual can alienate his liberty and turn himself into the slave of a master, why could not an entire people alienate their liberty and turn themselves into the subject of a king?[14] There are many equivocal words here that need explanation, but let us confine ourselves to

---

13. [Romans 13:1.]
14. [Grotius, *Law of War and Peace*, bk. 1, ch. 3, §12.]

the word *alienate*. To alienate is to give or to sell. A man who makes himself the slave of someone else does not give himself; he sells himself, at least for his subsistence. But why do a people sell themselves? Far from furnishing his subjects with their subsistence, a king derives his own from them alone, and, according to Rabelais, a king does not live cheaply. Do subjects then give their persons on the condition that their possessions will also be taken? I fail to see what remains for them to preserve.

It will be said that the despot assures his subjects of civil tranquility.[15] Very well. But what do they gain, if the wars his ambition drags them into, if his insatiable greed, if the oppressive demands caused by his ministers, occasion more grief for his subjects than their own dissensions would have done? What do they gain, if this very tranquility is one of their miseries? A tranquil life is also had in dungeons; is that enough to make them desirable? The Greeks who were locked up in the Cyclops' cave lived a tranquil existence as they awaited their turn to be devoured.[16]

To say that a man gives himself gratuitously is to say something absurd and inconceivable. Such an act is illegitimate and null, if only for the fact that he who commits it does not have his wits about him. To say the same thing of an entire people is to suppose a people composed of madmen. Madness does not make right.

Even if each person can alienate himself, he cannot alienate his children. They are born men and free. Their liberty belongs to them; they alone have the right to dispose of it. Before they have reached the age of reason, their father can, in their name, stipulate conditions for their preservation and for their well-being. But he cannot give them irrevocably and unconditionally, for such a gift is contrary to the ends of nature and goes beyond the rights of paternity. For an arbitrary government to be legitimate, it would therefore be necessary in each generation for the people to be master of its acceptance or rejection. But in that event, this government would no longer be arbitrary.

Renouncing one's liberty is renouncing one's dignity as a man, the rights of humanity, and even its duties. There is no possible compensation for anyone who renounces everything. Such a renunciation is incompatible with the nature of man. Taking away all liberty from his will is tantamount to removing all morality from his actions. Finally, it is a vain and contradictory agreement that stipulates absolute authority on one side and a limitless obedience on the other. Is it not clear that no commitments are made to a person from whom one has the right to demand everything? And does this

15. [This is what Hobbes would say.]
16. [Cf. Locke, *Two Treatises*, Second Treatise, §228.]

7

condition alone not bring with it, since there is no equivalent or exchange, the nullity of the act? For what right would my slave have against me, given that all he has belongs to me, and that, since his right is my right, my having a right against myself makes no sense?

Grotius and others[17] derive from war another origin for the alleged right of slavery. Since, according to them, the victor has the right to kill the vanquished, these latter can ransom their lives at the price of their liberty—a contract all the more legitimate since it turns a profit for both of them.

But clearly, this alleged right to kill the vanquished does not in any way derive from the state of war.[18] Men are not naturally enemies, for the simple reason that men living in their original state of independence do not have sufficiently constant relationships among themselves to bring about either a state of peace or a state of war. It is the relationship between things and not that between men that brings about war. And since this state of war cannot come into existence from simple personal relations, but only from real relations,[19] a private war between one man and another can exist neither in the state of nature, where there is no constant property, nor in the social state, where everything is under the authority of the laws.

Fights between private individuals, duels, and brawls are not acts that produce a state. And with regard to private wars, authorized by the ordinances of King Louis IX of France and suspended by The Peace of God, they are abuses peculiar to feudal government, an absurd system if there ever was one, contrary to the principles of natural right and to all sound polity.

War is not, therefore, a relationship between one man and another, but a relationship between one state and another. In war private individuals are enemies only incidentally—not as men or even as citizens[20] but as soldiers;

---

17. [Hobbes, *De Cive*, ch. 8, and Samuel Pufendorf, *Of the Law of Nature and Nations*, bk. 6, ch. 3.]

18. [See Rousseau's essay "The State of War" in *The Basic Political Writings*, 2nd ed. (Hackett, 2011), 255–65.]

19. ["Real" is used here in the same way that we talk about "real estate," i.e., real relations are proprietary relations.]

20. [At this point the following passage was added to the 1782 edition: "The Romans, who had a better understanding of and a greater respect for the right of war than any other nation, carried their scruples so far in this regard that a citizen was not allowed to serve as a volunteer unless he had expressly committed himself against the enemy and against a specifically named enemy. When a legion in which Cato the son first served had been reorganized, Cato the Elder wrote Popilius that if he wanted his son to continue to serve under him, he would have to make him swear the military oath afresh, since, with the first one having been annulled, he could no longer take up arms against the enemy. And this very same Cato wrote to his son

not as members of the homeland but as its defenders. Finally, each state can have as enemies only other states and not men, since there can be no real relationship between things of disparate natures.

This principle is even in conformity with the established maxims of all times and with the constant practice of all civilized peoples. Declarations of war are warnings not so much to powers as to their subjects. The foreigner (be he king, private individual, or a people) who robs, kills, or detains subjects of another prince without declaring war on the prince, is not an enemy but a brigand. Even in the midst of war, a just prince rightly appropriates to himself everything in an enemy country belonging to the public, but respects the person and goods of private individuals. He respects the rights upon which his own rights are founded. Since the purpose of war is the destruction of the enemy state, one has the right to kill the defenders of that state as long as they bear arms. But as soon as they lay down their arms and surrender, they cease to be enemies or instruments of the enemy. They return to being simply men; and one no longer has a right to their lives. Sometimes a state can be killed without a single one of its members being killed. For war does not grant a right that is unnecessary to its purpose.[21] These principles are not those of Grotius; they are not based on the authority of poets.[22] Rather they are derived from the nature of things; they are based on reason.

As to the right of conquest, the only basis it has is the law of the strongest. If war does not give the victor the right to massacre the vanquished peoples, this right (which he does not have) cannot be the basis for the right to enslave them. One has the right to kill the enemy only when one cannot enslave him. The right to enslave him does not therefore derive from the right to kill him. Hence, it is an iniquitous exchange to make him buy his life, to which no one has any right, at the price of his liberty. In establishing the right of life and death on the right of slavery, and the right of slavery on the right of life and death, is it not clear that one falls into a vicious circle?

Even if we were to suppose that there were this terrible right to kill everyone, I maintain that neither a person enslaved during wartime nor a conquered people bear any obligation whatever toward its master, except

---

to take care to avoid going into battle without swearing this military oath afresh. I know the siege of Clusium and other specific cases can be raised as counterexamples to this, but for my part I cite laws and customs. The Romans were the ones who transgressed their laws least often and are the only ones to have such noble laws."]
21. [Cf. Montesquieu, *Spirit of the Laws*, bk. 10, ch. 3.]
22. [An attack on Grotius, who repeatedly cites poets in the course of his argument.]

to obey him for as long as it is forced to do so. In taking the equivalent of his life, the victor has done him no favor. Instead of killing him unprofitably, he kills him usefully. Hence, far from the victor having acquired any authority over him beyond force, the state of war subsists between them just as before. Their relationship itself is the effect of war, and the usage of the right to war does not suppose any peace treaty. They have made a contract. Fine. But this contract, far from destroying the state of war, presupposes its continuation.

Thus, from every point of view, the right of slavery is null, not simply because it is illegitimate, but because it is absurd and meaningless. These words, *slavery* and *right*, are contradictory. They are mutually exclusive. Whether it is the statement of one man to another man, or of one man to a people, the following sort of talk will always be equally nonsensical: "I make an agreement with you that is wholly at your expense and wholly to my advantage; and, for as long as it pleases me, I will observe it and so will you."

Chapter 5

That It Is Always Necessary to Return to a First Agreement

Even if I were to grant all that I have thus far refuted, the supporters of despotism would not be any better off. There will always be a great difference between subduing a multitude and ruling a society. If scattered men were successively enslaved by a single individual, I see nothing there—however many they may be—but a master and slaves; I do not see a people and their leader. It is, if you will, an aggregation, but not an association. There is neither a public good nor a body politic there. Even if that man had enslaved half the world, he is always just a private individual. His interest, separated from that of others, is never anything but a private interest. If this same man happens to die, after his passing his empire remains scattered and disunited, just as an oak tree disintegrates and falls into a pile of ashes after fire has consumed it.

A people, says Grotius, can give themselves to a king. According to Grotius, therefore, a people are a people before they give themselves to a king. This gift itself is a civil act; it presupposes a public deliberation. Thus, before examining the act whereby a people choose a king, it would be well to examine the act whereby a people are a people. For since this act is necessarily prior to the other, it is the true foundation of society.

In fact, if there were no prior agreement, then, unless the vote were unanimous, what would be the basis of the minority's obligation to submit to the majority's choice, and where do one hundred who want a master get the right to vote on behalf of ten who do not? The law of majority rule is itself established by agreement and presupposes unanimity on at least one occasion.[23]

Chapter 6

On the Social Compact

I suppose that men have reached the point where obstacles that are harmful to their maintenance in the state of nature gain the upper hand by their resistance to the forces that each individual can bring to bear to maintain himself in that state. Such being the case, that original state cannot subsist any longer, and the human race would perish if it did not alter its mode of existence.

For since men cannot engender new forces, but merely unite and direct existing ones, they have no other means of maintaining themselves but to form by aggregation a sum of forces that could gain the upper hand over the resistance, so that their forces are directed by means of a single moving power and made to act in concert.

This sum of forces cannot come into being without the cooperation of many. But since each man's force and liberty are the primary instruments of his maintenance, how is he going to entrust them to others without hurting himself and without neglecting the care that he owes himself? This difficulty, seen in terms of my subject, can be stated in the following terms:

"Find a form of association that defends and protects with all common forces the person and goods of each associate, and, by means of which, each one, while uniting with all, nevertheless obeys only himself and remains as free as before." This is the fundamental problem for which the social contract provides the solution.

The clauses of this contract are so determined by the nature of the act that the least modification renders them vain and ineffectual, that, although perhaps they have never been formally promulgated, they are everywhere

---

23. [cf. Locke, *Two Treatises*, Second Treatise, ch. 8.]

the same, everywhere tacitly accepted and acknowledged. The result is that once the social compact is violated, each person then regains his first rights and resumes his natural liberty, while losing the contractual liberty[24] for which he renounced it.

These clauses, properly understood, are all reducible to a single one, namely, the total alienation of each associate together with all of his rights to the entire community. For first of all, since each person gives himself whole and entire, the condition is equal for everyone; and since the condition is equal for everyone, no one has an interest in making it burdensome for the others.

Moreover, since the alienation is made without reservation, the union is as perfect as possible, and no associate has anything further to demand. For if some rights remained with private individuals, in the absence of any common superior who could decide between them and the public, each person would eventually claim to be his own judge in all things, since he is on some particular point his own judge. The state of nature would subsist and the association would necessarily become tyrannical or hollow.

Finally, in giving himself to all, each person gives himself to no one. And since there is no associate over whom he does not acquire the same right that he would grant others over himself, he gains the equivalent of everything he loses, along with a greater amount of force to preserve what he has.

If, therefore, one eliminates from the social compact whatever is not essential to it, one will find that it is reducible to the following terms: *Each of us places his person and all his power in common under the supreme direction of the general will; and as one, we receive each member as an indivisible part of the whole.*

At once, in place of the individual person of each contracting party, this act of association produces a moral[25] and collective body composed of as many members as there are voices in the assembly, which receives from this same act its unity, its common *self*, its life, and its will. This public person, formed thus by union of all the others, formerly took the name *city*,[26] and

---

24. [Rousseau's phrase is *la liberté conventionelle.*]

25. [When Rousseau writes about a moral person, being, or body, he is using *moral* in a technical sense. In law a moral person is an entity capable of being legally responsible; corporations are therefore moral persons. This translation reproduces Rousseau's terminology, but one could often simply substitute "artificial" in order to grasp his sense.]

26. The true meaning of this word is almost entirely lost on modern men. Most of them mistake a town for a city and a townsman for a citizen. They do not know that houses make a town but citizens make a city. Once this mistake cost the

at present takes the name *republic* or *body politic*, which is called *state* by its members when it is passive, *sovereign* when it is active, *power* when compared to others like itself. As for the associates, they collectively take the name *people*; individually they are called *citizens*, insofar as they are participants in the sovereign authority, and *subjects*, insofar as they are subjected to the laws of the state. But these terms are often confused and mistaken for one another. It is enough to know how to distinguish them when they are used with absolute precision.

Chapter 7

On the Sovereign

This formula shows that the act of association includes a reciprocal commitment between the public and private individuals, and that each individual, contracting, as it were, with himself, finds himself under a twofold commitment, namely, as a member of the sovereign toward private individuals, and as a member of the state toward the sovereign. But the maxim of civil law that no one is held to commitments made to himself cannot be applied here, for there is a considerable difference between being obligated to oneself or to a whole of which one is a part.

It must be further noted that the public deliberation that can obligate all the subjects to the sovereign, owing to the two different relationships in which each of them is viewed, cannot, for the opposite reason, obligate the sovereign to itself and that consequently it is contrary to the nature of the

---

Carthaginians dearly. I have not found in my reading that the title of *citizen* has ever been given to the subjects of a prince, not even in ancient times to the Macedonians or in our own time to the English, although they are closer to liberty than all the others. Only the French adopt this name *citizen* with complete familiarity, since they have no true idea of its meaning, as can be seen from their dictionaries. If this were not the case, they would become guilty of treason for using it. For them, this name expresses a virtue and not a right. When Bodin wanted to speak about our citizens and townsmen, he committed a terrible blunder, for he mistook the one group for the other. Mr. d'Alembert was not in error, and in his article titled "Geneva" he has carefully distinguished the four orders of men (even five, counting ordinary foreigners) who are in our town [i.e., Geneva], and of whom only two make up the republic. No other French author I am aware of has grasped the true meaning of the word *citizen*. [Cf. Jean Bodin, *The Six Books of the Republic*, bk. 1, ch. 6.]

body politic that the sovereign impose upon itself a law it could not break. Since the sovereign can be considered under but one single relationship, it is then in the position of a private individual contracting with himself. Whence it is apparent that there neither is nor can be any type of fundamental law that is obligatory for the people as a body, not even the social contract.[27] This does not mean that the whole body cannot perfectly well commit itself to another body with respect to things that do not infringe on this contract. For in regard to the foreigner, it becomes a simple being, an individual.

However, since the body politic or the sovereign derives its being exclusively from the sanctity of the contract, it can never obligate itself, not even to another power, to do anything that derogates from the original act, such as alienating some portion of itself or submitting to another sovereign. Violation of the act whereby it exists would be self-annihilation, and whatever is nothing produces nothing.

As soon as this multitude is thus united in a body, one cannot harm one of the members without attacking the whole body. It is even less possible that the body can be harmed without the members feeling it. Thus duty and interest equally obligate the two contracting parties to come to one another's aid, and the same men should seek to combine in this twofold relationship all the advantages that result from it.

For since the sovereign is formed entirely from the private individuals who make it up, it neither has nor could have an interest contrary to theirs. Hence, the sovereign power has no need to offer a guarantee to its subjects, since it is impossible for a body to want to harm all of its members, and, as we will see later, it cannot harm any one of them in particular. The sovereign, by the mere fact that it exists, is always all that it should be.

But the same thing cannot be said of the subjects in relation to the sovereign, for whom, despite their common interest, their commitments would be without substance if it did not find ways of being assured of their fidelity.

In fact, each individual can, as a man, have a private will contrary to or different from the general will that he has as a citizen. His private interest can speak to him in an entirely different manner than the common interest. His absolute and naturally independent existence can cause him to envisage what he owes the common cause as a gratuitous contribution, the loss of which will be less harmful to others than its payment is burdensome to

---

27. [It is this argument, which undermines the notion of a constitution that must be preserved and respected, that led to Rousseau's book being condemned by the government of Geneva as destructive of all systems of government.]

him. And in viewing the moral person that constitutes the state as a theoretical entity[28] because it is not a man, he would enjoy the rights of a citizen without wanting to fulfill the duties of a subject, an injustice whose growth would bring about the ruin of the body politic.

Thus, in order for the social compact to avoid being an empty formula, it tacitly entails the commitment—which alone can give force to the others—that whoever refuses to obey the general will, will be forced to do so by the entire body. This means merely that he will be forced to be free. For it is this condition that, by giving each citizen to the homeland, guarantees him against all personal dependence, this condition that produces the skill and the performance of the political machine and that alone bestows legitimacy upon civil commitments. Without it, such commitments would be absurd, tyrannical, and subject to the worst abuses.

Chapter 8

On the Civil State

This passage from the state of nature to the civil state produces quite a remarkable change in man, for it substitutes justice for instinct in his behavior and gives his actions a moral quality they previously lacked. Only then, when the voice of duty replaces physical impulse and right replaces appetite, does man, who had hitherto taken only himself into account, find himself forced to act upon other principles and consult his reason before listening to his inclinations. Although in this state he deprives himself of several of the advantages belonging to him in the state of nature, he gains equally great ones in return. His faculties are exercised and developed, his ideas are broadened, his feelings are ennobled, his entire soul is elevated to such a height that, if the abuse of this new condition did not often lower his condition to beneath the level he left, he ought constantly to bless the happy moment that tore him away from it forever and that transformed him from a stupid, limited animal into an intelligent being and a man.

---

28. [Rousseau's term is *être de raison*, which corresponds to the scholastic *ens rationis*. Eighteenth-century dictionaries distinguish *êtres de raison* from *êtres réels*. This particular person—Tom Smith—or this particular dog—Fido—is real; humankind or the domesticated dog is an abstraction or *être de raison*.]

Let us summarize this entire balance sheet so that the credits and debits are easily compared. What man loses through the social contract is his natural liberty and an unlimited right to everything that tempts him and that he can acquire. What he gains is civil liberty and the proprietary ownership of all he possesses. So as not to be in error with regard to the value of these exchanges, it is necessary to draw a careful distinction between natural liberty (which is limited solely by the force of the individual involved) and civil liberty (which is limited by the general will), and between possession (which is merely the effect of force or of the right of the first occupant) and proprietary ownership (which can only be based on a positive title).

To the preceding could be added the acquisition in the civil state of moral liberty, which alone makes man truly the master of himself. For to be driven by appetite alone is slavery, and obedience to the law one has prescribed for oneself is liberty. But I have already said too much on this subject, and the philosophical meaning of the word *liberty* is not part of my subject here.

Chapter 9

On Real Property[29]

Each member of the community gives himself to it at the instant of its constitution, just as he actually is, himself and all his forces, including all the goods in his possession. This is not to say that by this act alone possession changes its nature as it changes hands and becomes property in the hands of the sovereign. Rather, since the forces of the city are incomparably greater than those of a private individual, public possession is by that very fact stronger and more irrevocable, without being more legitimate, at least to strangers. For with regard to its members, the state is master of all their goods in virtue of the social contract, which serves in the state as the basis of all rights. But with regard to other powers, the state is master only in virtue of the right of the first occupant, which it derives from private individuals.

The right of first occupant, though more real than the right of the strongest, does not become a true right until after the establishment of the right of property. Every man by nature has a right to everything he needs;

---

29. [Rousseau's title is *Du domaine réel.* "Real" refers to property in land (as in "real estate"), whereas *domaine* is a somewhat old-fashioned synonym for "property" but is used particularly for property in land.]

however, the positive act whereby he becomes a proprietor of some goods excludes him from all the rest. Once his lot has been determined, he should limit himself thereto, no longer having any right against the community. This is why the right of the first occupant, so weak in the state of nature, is able to command the respect of every man living in the civil state. In this right, one respects not so much what belongs to others as what does not belong to oneself.

In general, the following rules are necessary in order to authorize the right of the first occupant on any land. First, this land may not already be occupied by anyone. Second, no one may occupy more than the amount needed to subsist. Third, one is to take possession of it not by an empty ceremony, but by working and cultivating it—the only sign of property that ought, in the absence of legal titles, to be respected by others.[30]

In fact, by according the right of the first occupant only to those who need and who work, have we not extended it as far as it can go? Is it possible to avoid setting limits to this right? Will setting one's foot on a piece of common land be sufficient to claim it at once as one's own? Will having the force for a moment to drive off other men be sufficient to deny them the right ever to return? How can a man or a people seize a vast amount of territory and deprive the entire human race of it except by a punishable usurpation, since this seizure deprives all other men of the shelter and sustenance that nature gives them in common? When Nuñez Balboa stood on the shoreline and took possession of the South Sea and all of South America in the name of the crown of Castille, was this enough to dispossess all the inhabitants and to exclude all the princes of the world? On that basis, those ceremonies would be multiplied quite in vain. All the Catholic king had to do was take possession of the universe all at once from his study, excepting afterward from his empire only what already belonged to other princes.

One can imagine how the combined and contiguous lands of private individuals become public territory and how the right of sovereignty, extending from subjects to the land they occupy, becomes at once real and personal. This places its owners in a greater dependence, turning their very own forces into guarantees of their loyalty. This advantage does not seem to have been fully appreciated by the ancient monarchs, who, calling themselves merely kings of the Persians, the Scythians, and the Macedonians, appeared to regard themselves merely as the leaders of men rather than the masters of the country. Today's monarchs more shrewdly call themselves

---

30. [Rousseau here follows the chapter on property in Locke, *Two Treatises*, Second Treatise.]

kings of France, Spain, England, and so on. In holding the land thus, they are quite sure of holding the inhabitants.

What is remarkable about this alienation is that, in accepting the goods of private individuals, the community is far from despoiling them; rather, in so doing, it merely assures them of legitimate possession, changing usurpation into a true right, and enjoyment into proprietary ownership. So, since owners are considered trustees of the public good, and since their rights are respected by all members of the state and maintained with all its force against foreigners, through a surrender that is advantageous to the public and still more so to themselves, they have, so to speak, acquired all they have given. This paradox is easily explained by the distinction between the rights the sovereign and the proprietor have to the same land,[31] as will be seen later.

It can also happen that men begin to unite before possessing anything and later appropriate a piece of land sufficient for everyone, so that they enjoy it in common or divide it among themselves either in equal shares or according to proportions laid down by the sovereign. In whatever way this acquisition is accomplished, each private individual's right to his own land is always subordinate to the community's right to all, without which there could be neither solidity in the social fabric nor real force in the exercise of sovereignty.[32]

I will end this chapter and this book with a remark that should serve as a basis for every social system. It is that instead of destroying natural equality, the fundamental compact, on the contrary, substitutes a moral and legitimate equality to whatever physical inequality nature may have been able to impose upon men, and that, however unequal in force or intelligence they may be, men all become equal by agreement and by right.[33]

END OF THE FIRST BOOK

---

31. [Here and below, Rousseau writes *fond* but must mean *fonds*. The mistake seems to have been fairly common, but, as Jean-François Féraud points out in his *Dictionnaire critique de la langue française* of 1787–1788, *fond* means "bottom" (as in the bottom of a cup) whereas *fonds* means "land." They are two quite different words.]
32. [Cf. Hobbes, *De Cive*, ch. 12, §7.]
33. Under bad governments this equality is only apparent and illusory. It serves merely to maintain the poor man in his misery and the rich man in his usurpation. In actuality, laws are always useful to those who have possessions and harmful to those who have nothing. Whence it follows that the social state is advantageous to men only insofar as they all have something and none of them has too much.

BOOK II

Chapter 1

That Sovereignty Is Inalienable

The first and most important consequence of the principles established above is that only the general will can direct the forces of the state according to the purpose for which it was instituted, which is the common good. For if the opposition of private interests made necessary the establishment of societies, it is the accord of these same interests that made it possible. It is what these different interests have in common that forms the social bond, and, were there no point of agreement among all these interests, no society could exist. For it is utterly on the basis of this common interest that society ought to be governed.

I therefore maintain that since sovereignty is merely the exercise of the general will, it can never be alienated, and that the sovereign, which is only a collective being, cannot be represented by anything but itself. Power can perfectly well be transferred, but not the will.

In fact, while it is not impossible for a private will to be in accord on some point with the general will, it is impossible at least for this accord to be durable and constant. For by its nature the private will tends toward giving advantages to some and not to others, and the general will tends toward equality. It is even more impossible for there to be a guarantee of this accord even if it ought always to exist. This accord is not the result of art but of chance. The sovereign may well say, "Right now I want what a certain man wants or at least what he says he wants." But it cannot say, "What this man will want tomorrow I too will want," since it is absurd for the will to tie its hands for the future and since it is not within the capacity of any will to consent to anything contrary to the good of the being that wills. If, therefore, the people promise simply to obey, they dissolve themselves by this act; they lose their standing as a people. The very moment there is a master, there no longer is a sovereign, and thenceforward the body politic is destroyed.

This is not to say that the commands of the leaders could not pass for manifestations of the general will, as long as the sovereign, who is free to oppose them, does not do so. In such a case, the consent of the people ought to be presumed on the basis of universal silence. This will be explained at greater length.

Chapter 2

That Sovereignty Is Indivisible

Sovereignty is indivisible for the same reason that it is inalienable. For either the will is general[1] or it is not. It is the will of either the people as a whole or of only a part. In the first case, this will once declared is an act of sovereignty and constitutes law. In the second case, it is merely a private will, or an act of magistracy. At most it is a decree.

However, our political theorists, unable to divide sovereignty in its principle, divide it in its object. They divide it into force and will; into legislative and executive power; into rights of imposing taxes, of justice, and of war; into internal administration and power to negotiate with foreigners. Occasionally they mix all these parts together and sometimes they separate them. They turn the sovereign into a fantastic being made of bits and pieces. It is as if they built a man out of several bodies, one of which had eyes, another had arms, another feet, and nothing more. Japanese sleight-of-hand artists are said to dismember a child before the eyes of spectators, then, throwing all the parts in the air one after the other, they make the child fall back down alive and all in one piece. These conjuring acts of our political theorists are more or less like these performances. After having taken apart the social body by means of a sleight of hand worthy of a carnival, they put the pieces back together who knows how.

This error comes from not having formed precise notions of sovereign authority, and from having taken for parts of that authority what were merely emanations from it. Thus, for example, the acts of declaring war and making peace have been viewed as acts of sovereignty, which they are not, since each of these acts is not a law but merely an application of the law, a particular act determining the legal circumstances, as will be clearly seen when the idea attached to the word *law* comes to be defined.

In reviewing the other divisions in the same way, one would find that one is mistaken every time one believes one sees sovereignty divided, and that the

---

1. For a will to be general, it need not always be unanimous; however, it is necessary for all the votes to be counted. Any formal exclusion is a breach of generality.

rights one takes to be the parts of this sovereignty are all subordinated to it and always presuppose supreme wills that these rights merely put into effect.

It would be impossible to say how much this lack of precision has obscured the decisions of authors who have written about political right when they wanted to judge the respective rights of kings and peoples on the basis of the principles they had established. Anyone can see, in Chapters III and IV of Book I of Grotius, how this learned man and his translator, Barbeyrac, become entangled and caught up in their sophisms, for fear of either saying too much or too little according to their perspectives, and of offending the interests they needed to reconcile. Grotius, having taken refuge in France, unhappy with his homeland, and desirous of paying court to Louis XIII (to whom his book is dedicated) spares no pain to rob the people of all their rights and to invest kings with them by every possible artifice. This would also have been the wish of Barbeyrac, who dedicated his translation to King George I of England. But unfortunately, the expulsion of James II (which he calls an abdication) forced him to be evasive and on his guard and to beat around the bush, in order to avoid making William out to be a usurper.[2] If these two writers had adopted the true principles, all their difficulties would have been alleviated and they would always have been consistent. However, they would have reluctantly told the truth and found themselves paying court only to the people. For truth does not lead to success, and the people grant neither ambassadorships, nor university chairs, nor pensions.

Chapter 3

Whether the General Will Can Err

It follows from what has preceded that the general will is always right and always tends toward the public utility. However, it does not follow that the deliberations of the people always have the same degree of rectitude. We

---

2. [The Catholic James II was expelled from Britain in the revolution of 1688 and replaced by William and Mary. Rousseau is right to regard the word "abdication" as fundamental; it implies that no revolution had taken place and therefore implicitly denies a right of revolution. However, Jean Barbeyrac (1674–1744), who translated and edited Pufendorf, Grotius, and Cumberland, was more sympathetic to the arguments of Locke than Rousseau perhaps recognizes.]

always want what is good for us, but we do not always see what it is. The people are never corrupted, but they are often tricked, and only then do they appear to want what is bad.

There is often a great deal of difference between the will of all and the general will. The latter considers only the general interest, whereas the former considers private interest and is merely the sum of private wills. But remove from these same wills the pluses and minuses that cancel each other out,[3] and what remains as the sum of the differences is the general will.

If, when a sufficiently informed people deliberate, the citizens were to have no communication among themselves, the general will would always result from the large number of small differences, and the deliberation would always be good. But when intrigues and partial associations come into being at the expense of the large association, the will of each of these associations becomes general in relation to its members and particular in relation to the state. It can be said, then, that there are no longer as many voters as there are men, but merely as many as there are associations. The differences become less numerous and yield a result that is less general. Finally, when one of these associations is so large that it dominates all the others, the result is no longer a sum of minor differences, but a single difference. Then there is no longer a general will, and the opinion that dominates is merely a private opinion.

For the general will to be well articulated, it is therefore important that there should be no partial society in the state and that each citizen make up his own mind.[4] Such was the unique and sublime institution of the great Lycurgus. If there are partial societies, their number must be multiplied and inequality among them prevented, as was done by Solon, Numa,

---

3. "Each interest," says the Marquis d'Argenson [in *Considerations on the Former and Present Government of France*], "has different principles. The accord of two private interests is formed in opposition to that of a third." He could have added that the accord of all the interests is found in the opposition to that of each. If there were no different interests, the common interest, which would never encounter any obstacle, would scarcely be felt. Everything would proceed on its own and politics would cease being an art.

4. "It is true," says Machiavelli, "that some divisions are harmful to the republic while others are helpful to it. Those that are accompanied by sects and partisan factions are harmful while those are beneficial that maintain themselves without sects and partisan factions. Since, therefore, a ruler of a republic cannot prevent enmities from arising within it, he at least ought to prevent them from becoming sects," *The History of Florence*, Book VII. [Rousseau here quotes the Italian.]

and Servius.[5] These precautions are the only effective way of bringing it about that the general will is always enlightened and that the people do not deceive themselves.

Chapter 4

On the Limits of Sovereign Power

If the state or the city is merely a moral person whose life consists in the union of its members, and if the most important of its concerns is that of its own conservation, it ought to have a universal compulsory force to move and arrange each part in the manner best suited to the whole. Just as nature gives each man an absolute power over all his members, the social compact gives the body politic an absolute power over all its members, and it is the same power that, as I have said, is directed by the general will and bears the name *sovereignty*.

But over and above the public person, we need to consider the private persons who make it up and whose life and liberty are naturally independent of it. It is, therefore, a question of making a rigorous distinction between the respective rights of the citizens and the sovereign,[6] and between the duties the former have to fulfill as subjects and the natural right they should enjoy as men.

We grant that each person alienates, by the social compact, only that portion of his power, his goods, and liberty whose use is of consequence to the community;[7] but we must also grant that only the sovereign is the judge of what is of consequence.

A citizen should render to the state all the services he can as soon as the sovereign demands them. However, for its part, the sovereign cannot impose on the subjects any fetters that are of no use to the community. It

---

5. [Lycurgus was the author of the constitution of Sparta, Solon the key figure in the construction of Athenian democracy. Numa and Servius (the second and sixth kings of Rome) played crucial roles in the construction of Roman institutions; on Servius, see Book IV, Chapter 4.]

6. Attentive readers, please do not rush to accuse me of contradiction here. I have been unable to avoid it in my choice of words, given the poverty of the language. But wait.

7. [Rousseau agrees with Locke, *Two Treatises*, Second Treatise, ch. 8.]

cannot even will to do so, for under the law of reason nothing takes place without a cause, any more than under the law of nature.

The commitments that bind us to the body politic are obligatory only because they are mutual, and their nature is such that in fulfilling them one cannot work for someone else without also working for oneself. Why is the general will always right, and why do all constantly want the happiness of each of them, if not because everyone applies the word *each* to himself and thinks of himself as he votes for all? This proves that the equality of right and the notion of justice it produces are derived from the preference each person gives himself, and thus from the nature of man; that the general will, to be really such, must be general in its object as well as in its essence; that it must derive from all in order to be applied to all; and that it loses its natural rectitude when it tends toward any individual, determinate object. For then, judging what is foreign to us, we have no true principle of equity to guide us.

In effect, once it is a question of a state of affairs or a particular right concerning a point that has not been regulated by a prior, general agreement, the issue becomes contentious. It is a suit in which the interested private individuals are one of the parties and the public the other, but in which I fail to see either what law should be followed or what judge should render the decision. In these circumstances it would be ridiculous to want to appeal to an express decision of the general will, which can only be the conclusion reached by one of its parts, and which, for the other part, therefore, is merely an alien, particular will, inclined on this occasion to injustice and subject to error. Thus, just as a private will cannot represent the general will, the general will, for its part, alters its nature when it has a particular object; and, as general, it is unable to render a decision on either a man or a state of affairs. When, for example, the people of Athens appointed or dismissed their leaders, decreed that honors be bestowed on one or inflicted penalties on another, and by a multitude of particular decrees indiscriminately exercised all the acts of government, the people in this case no longer had a general will in the strict sense. It no longer functioned as sovereign but as magistrate.[8] This will appear contrary to commonly held opinions, but I must be given time to present my own.

---

8. [Rousseau's word is *magistrat*; but in eighteenth-century French, a "magistrate" can be someone who exercises justice (as with the English word) or someone responsible for what the French call *police*—a term that covers all measures to order a society— in other words, any member of the executive. Rousseau's examples cover both senses of the word. In modern French, one can say that the president of France is the first magistrate, which is to say only that he is the highest officer of the state. Thus Rousseau works with a bipartite classification—sovereign and magistrate—where

It should be seen from this that what makes the will general is not so much the number of votes as the common interest that unites them, for in this institution each person necessarily submits himself to the conditions he imposes on others, an admirable accord between interest and justice that bestows on common deliberations a quality of equity that disappears when any particular matter is discussed, for lack of a common interest uniting and identifying the reference point of the judge with that of the party.

From whatever viewpoint one approaches this principle, one always arrives at the same conclusion, namely that the social compact establishes among the citizens an equality of such a kind that they all commit themselves under the same conditions and should all enjoy the same rights. Thus by the very nature of the compact, every act of sovereignty (that is, every authentic act of the general will) obligates or favors all citizens equally, so that the sovereign knows only the nation as a body and does not draw distinctions between any of those members that make it up. Strictly speaking, then, what is an act of sovereignty? It is not an agreement between a superior and an inferior, but an agreement of the body with each of its members. This agreement is legitimate, because it has the social contract as a basis; equitable, because it is common to all; useful, because it can have only the general good for its object; and solid, because it has the public force and the supreme power as a guarantee. As long as the subjects are subordinated only to such agreement, they obey no one, but only obey their own will. And asking how far the respective rights of the sovereign and the citizens extend is asking how far the latter can commit themselves to one another, each to all and all to each.

We can see from this that the sovereign power, wholly absolute, sacred, and inviolable as it is, does not and cannot exceed the limits of general agreements, and that every man can completely dispose of such goods and freedom as has been left to him by these agreements. This results in the fact that the sovereign never has the right to lay more charges on one subject than on another, because in that case the matter becomes particular, and no longer within the range of the sovereign's competence.

Once these distinctions are granted, it is so false that there is, in the social contract, any genuine renunciation on the part of private individuals that their situation, as a result of this contract, is really preferable to what

we work with a tripartite classification—legislature (which represents the people, who are sovereign), executive, and judiciary. Since modern English terminology tends to draw a clear distinction between the executive and the judiciary, there is no convenient term in English that covers the range of the French term.]

it was beforehand; and, instead of an alienation, they have merely made an advantageous exchange of an uncertain and precarious mode of existence for another that is better and surer. Natural independence is exchanged for liberty; the power to harm others is exchanged for their own security; and their force, which others could overcome, for a right that the social union renders invincible. Their life itself, which they have devoted to the state, is continually protected by it; and when they risk their lives for its defense, what are they then doing but returning to the state what they have received from it? What are they doing, that they did not do more frequently and with greater danger in the state of nature, when they would inevitably have to fight battles, defending at the peril of their lives the means of their preservation? It is true that everyone has to fight, if necessary, for the homeland; but it also is the case that no one ever has to fight on his own behalf. Do we not still gain by running, for something that brings about our security, a portion of the risks we would have to run for ourselves once our security was taken away?

Chapter 5

On the Right of Life or Death

The question arises how private individuals who have no right to dispose of their own lives can transfer to the sovereign this very same right that they do not have. This question seems difficult to resolve only because it is poorly stated. Every man has the right to risk his own life in order to preserve it. Has it ever been said that a person who jumps out a window to escape a fire is guilty of committing suicide? Has this crime ever been imputed to someone who perishes in a storm, even though he was aware of the danger when he embarked?

The social treaty has as its purpose the conservation of the contracting parties. Whoever wills the end also wills the means, and these means are inseparable from some risks, even from some losses. Whoever wishes to preserve his life at the expense of others should also give it up for them when necessary. For the citizen is no longer judge of the peril to which the law wishes him to expose himself, and when the prince[9] has said to him,

---

9. [Rousseau explains the meaning he gives to the word *prince* in Book III, Chapter 1.]

"It is expedient for the state that you should die," he should die. Because it is under this condition alone that he has lived in security up to then, and because his life is no longer only a kindness of nature, but a conditional gift of the state.

The death penalty inflicted on criminals can be viewed from more or less the same point of view. It is in order to avoid being the victim of an assassin that a person consents to die if he were to become one. In making this treaty, far from disposing of one's own life, one thinks only of guaranteeing it. And it cannot be presumed that any of the contracting parties is then planning to get himself hanged.

Moreover, every malefactor who attacks the social right becomes through his transgressions a rebel and a traitor to the homeland; in violating its laws, he ceases to be a member, and he even wages war against it. In that case the preservation of the state is incompatible with his own. Thus one of the two must perish; and when the guilty party is put to death, it is less as a citizen than as an enemy. The legal proceeding and the judgment are the proofs and the declaration that he has broken the social treaty, and consequently that he is no longer a member of the state. For since he has acknowledged himself to be such, at least by his living there, he ought to be removed from it by exile as a violator of the compact, or by death as a public enemy. For such an enemy is not a moral person,[10] but a man, and in this situation the right of war is to kill the vanquished.[11]

But it will be said that the condemnation of a criminal is a particular act. Fine. So this condemnation is not a function of the sovereign. It is a right the sovereign can confer without itself being able to exercise it. All of my opinions are consistent, but I cannot present them all at once.

In addition, frequency of corporal punishment[12] is always a sign of weakness or of torpor in the government. There is no wicked man who could not

---

10. [Rousseau's term is *personne morale*, which we consistently translate as "moral person." But in normal usage the claim that a corporate entity is a moral person means that a corporate entity is *like* an individual human being (who is also a moral person) in that it can be held responsible for its actions. Here Rousseau uses *personne morale* to refer to a corporate entity *as opposed to* an individual human being. He is thus using *personne morale* as a technical term to refer to a corporate entity or an *artificial* being.]

11. [This is hard, even impossible, to reconcile with Rousseau's argument in Book I, Chapter 4.]

12. [Rousseau's term is *supplices*, which means corporal punishment. In *ancien régime* France, the standard punishments for crime were corporal—whipping, branding, breaking on the wheel, etc.—and so Rousseau does not intend to distinguish

be made good for something. One has the right to put to death, even as an example to others, only someone who cannot be preserved without danger.

With regard to the right of pardon, or of exempting a guilty party from the penalty decreed by the law and pronounced by the judge, this belongs only to one who is above the judge and the law, that is, to the sovereign. Still its right in this regard is not clearly defined, and the cases in which it is rightly used are truly rare. In a well-governed state, there are few punishments, not because many pardons are granted but because there are few criminals. When a state is in decline, the sheer number of crimes ensures impunity. Under the Roman Republic, neither the senate nor the consuls ever tried to grant pardons. The people themselves did not do so, although it sometimes revoked its own judgment. Frequent pardons indicate that transgressions will eventually have no need of them, and everyone sees where that leads. But I feel that my heart murmurs and holds back my pen. Let us leave these questions to be discussed by a just man who has not done wrong and who himself never needed pardon.

Chapter 6

On Law

Through the social compact, we have given existence and life to the body politic. It is now a matter of giving it movement and will through legislation. For the primitive act whereby this body is formed and united in no way determines what it should do to preserve itself.

Whatever is good and in conformity with order is such by the nature of things and independently of human agreements. All justice comes from God; he alone is its source. But if we knew how to receive it from so exalted a source, we would have no need for government or laws. Undoubtedly there is a universal justice emanating from reason alone; but this justice, to be admitted among us, ought to be reciprocal. Considering things from a human standpoint, the lack of a natural sanction causes the laws of justice to be without teeth among men. They do nothing but good to the wicked and evil to the just, when the latter observes them in his dealings with everyone

---

between corporal punishment and noncorporal punishment (prison, for example) but to refer to judicial punishments in general.]

while no one observes them in their dealings with him. There must therefore be agreements and laws to unite rights and duties and refer justice back to its object. In the state of nature where everything is commonly held, I owe nothing to those to whom I have promised nothing. I recognize as belonging to someone else only what is not useful to me. It is not this way in the civil state where all rights are fixed by law.

But what then, to get to the point, is a law? As long as we continue to be satisfied with attaching only metaphysical ideas to this word,[13] we will continue to reason without understanding each other. And when we have declared what a law of nature is, we will not thereby have a better grasp of what a law of the state is.

I have already stated that there is no general will concerning a particular object. In effect, this particular object is either within or outside of the state. If it is outside of the state, a will that is foreign to it is not general in relation to it. And if this object is within the state, that object is part of it; in that case, a relationship is formed between the whole and its parts that makes two separate beings, one of which is the part, and the other is the whole less that same part. But the whole less a part is not the whole, and as long as this relationship is the case, there is no longer a whole but rather two unequal parts. Whence it follows that the will of the one is certainly not general in relation to the other.

But when the entire people enact a statute concerning the entire people, they consider only themselves, and if in that case a relationship is formed, it is between the entire object seen from one perspective and the entire object seen from another, without any division of the whole. Then the subject matter about which a statute is enacted is general like the will that enacts it. It is this act that I call a law.

When I say that the object of the laws is always general, I have in mind that the law considers subjects as a body and actions in the abstract, never a man as an individual or a particular action. Thus the law can perfectly well enact a statute to the effect that there be privileges, but it cannot bestow them by name on anyone. The law can create several classes of citizens, and even stipulate the qualifications that determine membership in these classes, but it cannot name specific persons to be admitted to them. It can establish a royal government and a hereditary line of succession, but it cannot elect a king or name a royal family. In a word, any function that relates to an individual does not belong to the legislative power.

On this view, it is immediately obvious that it is no longer necessary to ask who is to make the laws, since they are the acts of the general will; nor

13. [Rousseau is attacking Montesquieu, *Spirit of the Laws*, bk. 1, ch. 1.]

whether the prince is above the laws, since he is a member of the state; nor whether the law can be unjust, since no one is unjust to himself; nor how one is both free and subject to the laws, since they are merely the record of our own wills.

Moreover, it is apparent that since the law combines the universality of the will and that of the object, what a man, whoever he may be, decrees on his own authority is not a law. What even the sovereign decrees concerning a particular object is no closer to being a law; rather, it is a decree. Nor is it an act of sovereignty but of magistracy.

I therefore call every state ruled by laws a republic, regardless of the form its administration may take.[14] For only then does the public interest govern, and only then is the "public thing" [in Latin: *res publica*] something real. Every legitimate government is republican.[15] I will explain later on what government is.

Strictly speaking, laws are merely the conditions of civil association. The people that are subjected to the laws ought to be their author. The regulating of the conditions of a society belongs to no one but those who are in association with one another. But how will they regulate these conditions? Will it be by a common accord, by a sudden inspiration? Does the body politic have an organ for making known its will? Who will give it the necessary foresight to formulate acts and to promulgate them in advance, or how will it announce them in time of need? How will a blind multitude, which often does not know what it wants (since it rarely knows what is good for it), carry out on its own an enterprise as great and as difficult as a system of legislation? By themselves the people always want the good, but by themselves they do not always see it. The general will is always right, but the judgment that guides it is not always enlightened. It must be made to see objects as they are, and sometimes as they ought to appear to it. The good path it seeks must be pointed out to it. It must be made safe from the seduction of private wills.

---

14. [As Rousseau goes on to explain, by his definition a monarchy can be a republic. Rousseau's definition of "republic" as any legitimate government was becoming unusual (in Montesquieu, for example, republic is an antonym of monarchy), but it had been until recently the standard definition—thus Bodin's *Six Books of the Republic* is about legitimate government in general and not about "republics" in the modern, Montesquieuian sense—and it corresponds to classical usage.]

15. By this word I do not have in mind merely an aristocracy or a democracy, but in general every government guided by the general will, which is the law. To be legitimate, the government need not be made indistinguishable from the sovereign, but it must be its servant. Then the monarchy itself is a republic. This will become clear in the next Book.

It must be given a sense of time and place. It must weigh present, tangible advantages against the danger of distant, hidden evils. Private individuals see the good they reject. The public wills the good that it does not see. Everyone is equally in need of guides. The former must be obligated to conform their wills to their reason; the latter must learn to know what it wants. Then public enlightenment results in the union of the understanding and the will in the social body—hence, the full cooperation of the parts and finally the greatest force of the whole. Whence there arises the necessity of having a legislator.

Chapter 7

On the Legislator

Discovering the rules of society best suited to nations would require a superior intelligence that beheld all the passions of men without feeling any of them; who had no affinity with our nature, yet knew it through and through; whose happiness was independent of us, yet who nevertheless was willing to concern itself with ours; finally, who, in the passage of time, procures for himself a distant glory, being able to labor in one age and obtain his reward in another.[16] Gods would be needed to give men laws.

The same reasoning used by Caligula[17] in practice was used by Plato when dealing with questions of principle in order to define the civil[18] or royal man he looks for in his dialogue *The Statesman*. But if it is true that a great prince is a rare man, what about a great legislator? The former merely has to follow the model the latter should propose to him. The latter is the engineer who invents the machine; the former is merely the workman who constructs it and makes it run. "At the birth of societies," says Montesquieu, "it is the leaders of republics who bring about the institution, and thereafter it is the institution that forms the leaders of republics."[19]

---

16. A people never becomes famous except when their legislation begins to decline. It is not known for how many centuries the constitution established by Lycurgus caused the happiness of the Spartans before the rest of Greece took note of it.
17. [That kings are gods.]
18. [Rousseau is using *civil* here to mean "fit to be a citizen." In Latin *civilis* is the adjective from *civis*, "citizen."]
19. [The quotation comes from Montesquieu's *Considerations on the Causes of the Greatness of the Romans and Their Decline*, ch. 1.]

He who dares to undertake the establishment of a people should feel that he is, so to speak, in a position to change human nature, to transform each individual (who by himself is a perfect and solitary whole) into a part of a larger whole from which this individual receives, in a sense, his life and his being; to alter man's constitution in order to strengthen it; to substitute a partial and moral existence for the physical and independent existence we have all received from nature. In a word, he must deny man his own forces in order to give him forces that are alien to him and that he cannot make use of without the help of others. The more these natural forces are dead and obliterated, and the greater and more durable are the acquired forces, the more too is the constitution solid and perfect. Thus if each citizen is nothing and can do nothing except in concert with all the others, and if the force acquired by the whole is equal or superior to the sum of the natural forces of all the individuals, one can say that the legislation has achieved the highest possible point of perfection.

The legislator is in every respect an extraordinary man in the state.[20] If he ought to be so by his genius, he is no less so by his office, which is neither magistracy nor sovereignty. This office, which constitutes the republic, does not enter into its constitution. It is a particular and superior function having nothing in common with the dominion over men. For if he who has command over men must not have command over laws, he who has command over the laws must no longer have any authority over men. Otherwise, his laws, ministers of his passions, would often only serve to perpetuate his injustices, and he could never avoid specific judgments altering the sanctity of his work.

When Lycurgus gave laws to his homeland, he began by abdicating the throne. It was the custom of most Greek cities to entrust the establishment of their laws to foreigners. The modern republics of Italy often imitated this custom. The Republic of Geneva did the same and things worked out well.[21] In its finest age Rome saw the revival within its midst of all the crimes of tyranny and saw itself on the verge of perishing as a result of having united the legislative authority and the sovereign power in the same hands.

---

20. [See Machiavelli, *Discourses*, bk. 1, chs. 9–10.]

21. Those who view Calvin simply as a theologian fail to grasp the extent of his genius. The codification of our wise edicts, in which he had a large role, does him as much honor as his *Institutes*. Whatever revolution time may bring out in our religious worship, as long as the love of homeland and of liberty is not extinguished among us, the memory of this great man will never cease to be held sacred.

Nevertheless, the decemvirs[22] themselves never claimed the right to have any law passed on their authority alone. "Nothing we propose," they would tell the people, "can become law without your consent. Romans, be yourselves the authors of the laws that should bring about your happiness."

He who drafts the laws, therefore, does not or should not have any legislative right. And the people themselves cannot, even if they wanted to, deprive themselves of this incommunicable right, because, according to the fundamental compact, only the general will obligates private individuals, and there can never be any assurance that a private will is in conformity with the general will until it has been submitted to the free vote of the people. I have already said this, but it is not a waste of time to repeat it.

Thus we find together in the work of legislation two things that seem incompatible: an undertaking that transcends human capacities and, to execute it, an authority that is nil.

Another difficulty deserves attention. The wise men who want to speak to the common masses in the former's own language rather than in the common vernacular cannot be understood by the masses. For there are a thousand kinds of ideas that are impossible to translate into the language of the people. Overly general perspectives and overly distant objects are equally beyond their grasp. Each individual, in having no appreciation for any other plan of government but the one that relates to his own private interest, finds it difficult to realize the advantages he ought to draw from the continual privations that good laws impose. For an emerging people to be capable of appreciating the sound maxims of politics and of following the fundamental rules of statecraft, the effect would have to become the cause. The social spirit that ought to be the work of that constitution would have to preside over the writing of the constitution itself. And men would be, prior to the advent of laws, what they ought to become by means of laws. Since, therefore, the legislator is incapable of using either force or reasoning, he must of necessity have recourse to an authority of a different order, which can compel without violence and persuade without convincing.

This is what has always forced the fathers of nations to have recourse to the intervention of heaven and to credit the gods with their own wisdom, so that the peoples, subjected to the laws of the state as to those of nature and

---

22. [A committee of ten established in the Roman Republic for the first time in 451 BC to reform the laws.]

recognizing the same power in the formation of man and of the city, might obey with liberty and bear with docility the yoke of public felicity.

It is this sublime reason, which transcends the grasp of ordinary men, whose decisions the legislator puts in the mouth of the immortals in order to compel by divine authority those whom human prudence could not move.[23] But not everybody is capable of making the gods speak or of being believed when he proclaims himself their interpreter. The great soul of the legislator is the true miracle that should prove his mission. Any man can engrave stone tablets, buy an oracle, or feign secret intercourse with some divinity, or train a bird to talk in his ear, or find other crude methods of imposing his beliefs on the people. He who knows no more than this may perchance assemble a troupe of lunatics, but he will never found an empire and his extravagant work will soon die with him. Pointless sleights of hand form a fleeting connection; only wisdom can make it lasting. The Judaic law, which still exists, and that of the child of Ishmael,[24] which has ruled half the world for ten centuries, still proclaim today the great men who enunciated them. And while pride-ridden philosophy or the blind spirit of factionalism sees in them nothing but lucky impostors, the true political theoretician admires in their institutions that great and powerful genius which presides over establishments that endure.

We should not, with Warburton,[25] conclude from this that politics and religion have a common object among us, but that in the beginning stages of nations the one serves as an instrument of the other.

---

23. "And in truth," says Machiavelli, "there has never been among a people a single legislator who, in proposing extraordinary laws, did not have recourse to God, for otherwise they would not be accepted, since there are many benefits known to a prudent man that do not have in themselves evident reasons enabling them to persuade others." *Discourses on Titus Livy*, Book I, Ch. XI. [Rousseau here quotes the Italian.]
24. [Kedar, held to be an ancestor of Muhammad.]
25. [Bishop William Warburton (1698–1779), author of *The Alliance between Church and State* (1736, translated into French in 1742) and *The Divine Legation of Moses* (1738–1741).]

Chapter 8

On the People[26]

Just as an architect, before putting up a large building, surveys and tests the ground to see if it can bear the weight, the wise teacher does not begin by laying down laws that are good in themselves. Rather he first examines whether the people for whom they are destined are fitted to bear them. For this reason, Plato refused to give laws to the Arcadians and to the Cyrenians, knowing that these two peoples were rich and could not abide equality. For this reason, one finds good laws and evil men in Crete, because Minos had disciplined nothing but a vice-ridden people.

A thousand nations have achieved brilliant earthly success that could never have abided good laws; and even those that could have would have been able to have done so for a very short period of their entire existence. Peoples,[27] like men, are docile only in their youth. As they grow older they become incorrigible. Once customs are established and prejudices have become deeply rooted, it is a dangerous and vain undertaking to want to reform them. The people cannot abide having even their evils touched in order to eliminate them, just like those stupid and cowardly patients who quiver at the sight of a physician.

This is not to say that, just as certain maladies unhinge men's minds and remove from them the memory of the past, one does not likewise sometimes find in the period during which states have existed violent epochs when revolutions do to peoples what certain crises do to individuals, when the horror of the past takes the place of forgetfulness, and when the state, set afire by civil wars, is reborn, as it were, from its ashes and takes on again the vigor of youth as it escapes death's embrace. Such was

---

26. [There is an important difference between *le peuple* in French and "the people" in English. In French *le peuple* is a singular noun which takes a singular verb. In English "the people" can be a singular noun or a plural noun ("the Roman people"; "the people over there"), but in modern English it always takes a plural verb: "The Roman people *are* proud of *their* history." In French one would say, in effect, "The Roman people is proud of its history," and it may thus be easier in French to think of the people as having a collective identity, as we think of nations: we write, "The English nation is proud of its history," not "The English nation are proud of their history."]

27. [In the 1782 edition, this sentence was revised to read, "Most peoples, like men. ..."]

Sparta at the time of Lycurgus; such was Rome after the Tarquins; and such in our time have been Holland and Switzerland after the expulsion of the tyrants. But these events are rare. They are exceptions whose cause is always to be found in the particular constitution of the states in question. They cannot take place even twice to the same people, for they can make themselves free as long as they are merely barbarous; but they can no longer do so when civil strength is exhausted. At that point internal conflicts can destroy the people with revolutions being unable to reestablish them. And as soon as their chains are broken, the people fall apart and they exist no longer. Henceforward a master is needed, not a liberator. Free peoples, remember this axiom: liberty can be acquired, but it can never be recovered.

For nations, as for men, there is a time of maturity that must be awaited before subjecting them to the laws.[28] But the maturity of a people is not always easily recognized; and if it is anticipated, the work is ruined. One people lend themselves to discipline at their inception; another, not even after ten centuries. The Russians will never be truly civilized, since they have been civilized too early. Peter had a genius for imitation.[29] He did not have true genius, the kind that creates and makes everything out of nothing. Some of the things he did were good; most of them were out of place. He saw that his people were barbarous; he did not see that they were not ready for civilization. He wanted to civilize them when all they needed was toughening. He wanted to begin by making Germans and Englishmen, when he should have started by making Russians. He prevented his subjects from ever becoming what they could have been by persuading them that they were something they are not. This is exactly how a French tutor trains his pupil to shine for a short time in his childhood, and afterward never to amount to a thing. The Russian Empire would like to subjugate Europe and will itself be subjugated. The Tartars, its subjects or its neighbors, will become its masters and ours. This revolution appears inevitable to me. All the kings of Europe are working in concert to hasten its occurrence.

---

28. [In the 1782 edition, this sentence was revised to read, "Youth is not childhood. For nations, as for men, maturity must be awaited. . . ."]
29. [Peter the Great (1672–1725), who had been praised by Voltaire in his *History of the Russian Empire under Peter the Great* (1759–1763).]

Chapter 9

The People (continued)

Just as nature has set limits to the stature of a well-formed man, beyond which there are but giants or dwarfs, so too, with regard to the best constitution of a state, there are limits to the size it can have, so as not to be too large to be capable of being well governed, nor too small to be capable of preserving itself on its own. In every body politic there is a *maximum* force that it cannot exceed and that it often falls short of by increasing in size. The more the social bond extends the looser it becomes, and in general a small state is proportionately stronger than a large one.

A thousand reasons prove this maxim. First, administration becomes more difficult over great distances, just as a weight becomes heavier at the end of a longer lever. It also becomes more onerous as the number of administrative levels multiplies, because first each city has its own administration that the people pay for; each district has its own, again paid for by the people; next each province has one and then the great governments, the satrapies, and vice royalties, requiring a greater cost the higher you go and always at the expense of the unfortunate people. Finally, there is the supreme administration that crushes everyone. All these surcharges continually exhaust the subjects. Far from being better governed by these different orders, they are worse governed than if there were but one administration over them. Meanwhile, hardly any resources remain for meeting emergencies; and when recourse must be made to them, the state is always on the verge of its ruin.

This is not all. Not only does the government have less vigor and quickness in enforcing the observance of the laws, preventing nuisances, correcting abuses, and foreseeing the seditious undertakings that can occur in distant places, but also the people have less affection for their leaders when it never sees them, for the homeland, which, to their eyes, is like the world, and for their fellow citizens, the majority of whom are foreigners to them. The same laws cannot be suitable to so many diverse provinces that have different customs, live in contrasting climates, and are incapable of enduring the same form of government. Different laws create only trouble and confusion among peoples who live under the same rulers and are in continuous communication. They intermingle and intermarry and, being under the sway of other customs, never know whether their patrimony is actually their own. Talents are hidden; virtues are unknown; vices are unpunished in this multitude of men who are unknown to one another and who are brought together in one place by the seat of supreme administration. The leaders, overwhelmed with work, see nothing for themselves; clerks govern the state. Finally, the measures that need to be taken to maintain the general authority, which so many distant officials want to avoid or mislead, absorb all the public attention. Nothing more remains for the people's happiness, and there barely remains enough for their defense in time of need. And thus a body that is too big for its constitution collapses and perishes, crushed by its own weight.

On the other hand, the state ought to provide itself with a firm foundation to give it solidity, to resist the shocks it is bound to experience, as well as the efforts it will have to make to sustain itself. For all the peoples have a kind of centrifugal force, by which they continually act one against the other and tend to expand at the expense of their neighbors, like Descartes' vortices. Thus the weak risk being soon swallowed up; scarcely any people can preserve themselves except by putting themselves in a kind of equilibrium with all, which nearly equalizes the pressure on all sides.

It is clear from this that there are reasons for expanding and reasons for contracting, and it is not the least of the statesman's talents to find, between the arguments on the one side and the arguments on the other, the proportion most advantageous to the preservation of the state. In general, it can be said that the former reasons, being merely external and relative, should be subordinated to the latter reasons, which are internal and absolute. A strong, healthy constitution is the first thing one needs to look for, and one should count more on the vigor born of a good government than on the resources furnished by a large territory.

Moreover, there have been states so constituted that the necessity for conquests entered into their very constitution and that, to maintain themselves, they were forced to expand endlessly. Perhaps they congratulated themselves greatly on account of this happy necessity, which nevertheless showed them, together with the limit of their size, the inevitable moment of their fall.

Chapter 10

The People (continued)

A body politic can be measured in two ways, namely, by the size of its territory and by the number of its people. And between these measurements, there is a relationship suitable for giving the state its true greatness. Men are what make up the state, and land is what feeds men. This relationship therefore consists in there being enough land for the maintenance of its inhabitants and as many inhabitants as the land can feed. It is in this proportion that the *maximum* force of a given population size is found. For if there is too much land, its defense is onerous, its cultivation inadequate, and its yield overabundant. This is the proximate cause of defensive wars. If there is not enough land, the state finds itself at the discretion of its neighbors for what it needs as a supplement. This is the proximate cause of offensive wars. Any people whose position provides them no alternative other than between commerce and war are inherently weak. They depend on their neighbors; they depend on events. They never have anything but an uncertain and brief existence. Either they conquer and change the situation or they are conquered and obliterated. They can keep themselves free only by shrinking or expanding.

No one can provide in mathematical terms a fixed relationship between the size of land and the population size that are sufficient for one another, as much because of the differences in the characteristics of the terrain, its degrees of fertility, the nature of its crops, the influence of its climates, as because of the differences to be noted in the temperaments of the men who inhabit the different countries, some of whom consume little in a fertile country, while others consume a great deal on a barren soil. Again, attention must be given to the greater or lesser fertility of women, to what the country can offer that is more or less favorable to the population, to the number of people that the legislator can hope to bring together there through what he establishes. Thus, the legislator should not base his judgment on what he sees but on what he foresees. And he should dwell less upon the present state of the population than upon the state it should naturally attain. Finally, there are a thousand situations where the idiosyncrasies of a place require or permit the acquisition of more land than appears necessary. Thus, there needs to be considerable expansion in mountainous country, where the natural crops—namely, woods and pastures—demand less work; where experience shows that women are more fertile than on the plains; and where a large amount of sloping soil is the equivalent of only a very small amount of flat land, for it is the horizontal section which matters when predicting yields. On the other hand, people can draw closer to one another at the seashore, even on rocks and nearly barren sand, since fishing can make up to a great degree for the lack of land crops, since men should be more closely gathered together in order to repulse pirates, and since in addition it is easier to unburden the country of surplus inhabitants by means of colonies.

To these conditions for instituting a people must be added one that cannot be a substitute for any other, but without which all the rest are useless: the enjoyment of prosperity and of peace. For the time when a state is being organized, like the time when a battalion is being formed, is the instant when the body is the least capable of resisting and the easiest to destroy. There would be better resistance at a time of absolute disorder than at a moment of fermentation, when each man is occupied with establishing his own position rather than with the danger. Were a war, famine, or sedition to arise in this time of crisis, the state inevitably would be overthrown.

This is not to say that many governments are not established during such storms; but in these instances it is these governments themselves that destroy the state. Usurpers always bring about or choose these times of conflict to use public terror to pass destructive laws that the people would never adopt if they had their composure. The choice of the moment at which a government is to be instituted is one of the surest signs by which the work of a legislator can be distinguished from that of a tyrant.

What people, therefore, are suited for legislation? A people that, finding themselves bound by some union of origin, interest, or agreement, have not yet felt the true yoke of laws. One that have no customs or superstitions that are deeply rooted. One that do not fear being overpowered by sudden invasion. One that can, without entering into the squabbles of its neighbors, resist each of them single-handed or use the help of one to repel another. One where each member can be known to all, and where there is no need to impose a greater burden on a man than a man can bear. One that can get along without other peoples and without which every other people can get along.[30] One that is neither rich nor poor and can be sufficient unto itself; finally, one that brings together the stability of an ancient people and the docility of a new people. What makes the work of legislation trying is not so much what must be established as what must be destroyed. And what makes success so rare is the impossibility of finding the simplicity of nature together with the needs of society. All these conditions, it is true, are hard to find in combination. Hence few well-constituted states are to be seen.

---

30. If there were two neighboring peoples, one being unable to get along without the other, it would be a very tough situation for the former and very dangerous for the latter. In such a case, every wise nation will work very quickly to free the other of its dependency. The Republic of Tlaxcala, enclosed within the Mexican Empire, preferred to do without salt rather than buy it from the Mexicans or even be given it by them without charge. The wise Tlaxcalans saw the trap hidden beneath this generosity. They kept themselves free, and this small state, enclosed within this great empire, was finally the instrument of its ruin.

In Europe there is still one country capable of receiving legislation. It is the island of Corsica. The valor and constancy with which these brave people have regained and defended their liberty would well merit having some wise man teach them how to preserve it. I have a feeling that someday that little island will astonish Europe.

Chapter 11

On the Various Systems of Legislation

If one enquires into precisely wherein the greatest good of all consists, which should be the purpose of every system of legislation, one will find that it boils down to these two principal objects, *liberty* and *equality*. Liberty, because all personal dependence is that much force taken from the body of the state; equality, because liberty cannot subsist without it.

I have already said what civil liberty is. Regarding equality, we need not mean by this word that degrees of power and of wealth are to be absolutely the same, but rather that, with regard to power, it should fall short of any violence and never be exercised except by virtue of rank and laws; and, with regard to wealth, no citizen should be so rich as to be capable of buying another citizen, and none so poor that he is forced to sell himself. This presupposes moderation in goods and power on the part of the great, and moderation in avarice and covetousness[31] on the part of the lowly.

This equality is said to be a speculative fiction that cannot exist in practice. But if abuse is inevitable, does it follow that it should not at least be regulated? It is precisely because the force of things tends always to destroy equality that the force of legislation should always tend to maintain it.

But these general objectives of every good institution should be modified in each country in accordance with the relationships that arise as much from the local situation as from the temperament of the inhabitants. And it is on the basis of these relationships that each people must be assigned a particular institutional system that is the best, not perhaps in itself, but for

---

31. Do you therefore want to give stability to the state? Bring the extremes as close together as possible. Tolerate neither rich men nor beggars. These two estates, which are naturally inseparable, are equally fatal to the common good. From one come the supporters of tyranny, and from the other the tyrants. It is always between them that public liberty becomes a matter of commerce. The one buys it and the other sells it.

the state for which it is destined. For example, is the soil barren and unproductive, or the country too confining for its inhabitants? Turn to industry and arts,[32] whose products you will exchange for the foodstuffs you lack. On the contrary, do you live in rich plains and fertile slopes? Do you have a good terrain, but lack inhabitants? Put all your effort into agriculture, which increases the number of men, and chase out the arts that would only bring about the depopulation of the countryside by causing the few inhabitants that there are to flock together around a few points within the whole territory.[33] Do you occupy extensive, convenient coastlines? Cover the sea with vessels; cultivate commerce and navigation. You will have a brilliant and brief existence. Does the sea wash against nothing on your coasts but virtually inaccessible rocks? Remain barbarous and fish-eating. You will live in greater tranquility, better perhaps and certainly happily. In a word, aside from the maxims common to all, each people have within themselves some cause that organizes them in a particular way and renders their legislation proper for them alone. Thus it was that long ago the Hebrews and recently the Arabs have had religion as their main objective; the Athenians had letters; Carthage and Tyre, commerce; Rhodes, seafaring; Sparta, war; and Rome, virtue. The author of *The Spirit of the Laws*[34] has shown with a large array of examples the art by which the legislator directs the institution toward each of its objectives.

What makes the constitution of a state truly solid and lasting is that proprieties are observed with such fidelity that the natural relations and the laws are always in agreement on the same points and that the latter serve only to assure, accompany, and rectify the former. But if the legislator is mistaken about his object and takes a principle different from the one arising from the nature of things (whether the one tends toward servitude and the other toward liberty; the one toward riches, the other toward increased population; the one toward peace, the other toward conquests), the laws will weaken imperceptibly, the constitution will be altered, and the state will not cease being agitated until it is destroyed or changed, and invincible nature has regained her empire.

---

32. [Rousseau's word *arts* means "crafts" here but is translated as "arts" throughout for consistency.]
33. Any branch of foreign trade, says the Marquis d'Argenson, creates hardly anything more than a false utility for a kingdom in general. It can enrich some private individuals, even some towns, but the nation as a whole gains nothing and the people are none the better for it.
34. [Montesquieu, *Spirit of the Laws*, bk. 11, ch. 5.]

Chapter 12

Classification of the Laws

To set the whole in order or to give the commonwealth the best possible form, there are various relations to consider. First, the action of the entire body acting upon itself, that is, the relationship of the whole to the whole or of the sovereign to the state, and this relationship, as we shall see later, is composed of relationships of intermediate terms.

The laws regulating this relationship bear the name *political laws* and are also called *fundamental laws*, not without reason if these laws are wise. For if there is only one good way of organizing each state, the people who have found it should stand by it. But if the established order is evil, why should one accept as fundamental laws that prevent it from being good? Besides, a people are in any case always in a position to change their laws, even the best laws. For if they wish to do themselves harm, who has the right to prevent them from doing so?

The second relation is that of the members to each other or to the entire body. And this relationship should be as small as possible in regard to the former and as large as possible in regard to the latter, so that each citizen would be perfectly independent of all the others and excessively dependent upon the city. This always takes place by the same means, for only the force of the state brings about the liberty of its members. It is from this second relationship that civil laws arise.

We may consider a third sort of relation between man and law, namely, that of disobedience and penalty. And this gives rise to the establishment of criminal laws, which basically are not so much a particular kind of law as the sanction for all the others.

To these three sorts of law is added a fourth, the most important of all. It is not engraved on marble or bronze, but in the hearts of citizens. It is the true constitution of the state. Every day it takes on new forces. When other laws grow old and die away, it revives and replaces them, preserves a people in the spirit of their institution, and imperceptibly substitutes the force of habit for that of authority. I am speaking of mores, customs, and especially of opinion, a part of the law unknown to our statesmen but one on which depends the success of all the others:[35] a part with which the great legislator

---

35. [Pierre Bayle was the first to stress the importance of the law of opinion in maintaining social order in his *Diverse Thoughts on the Comet* (1682).]

secretly occupies himself, though he seems to confine himself to the particular regulations that are merely the arching of the vault, whereas mores, slower to arise, form in the end its immovable keystone.

Among these various classes, only political laws, which constitute the form of government, are relevant to my subject.

END OF THE SECOND BOOK

BOOK III

Before speaking of the various forms of government, let us try to determine the precise meaning of this word, which has not as yet been explained very well.

Chapter 1

On Government in General

I am warning the reader that this chapter should be read carefully and that I do not know the art of being clear to those who do not want to be attentive.

Every free action has two causes that come together to produce it. The one is moral, namely, the will that determines the act; the other is physical, namely, the power that executes it. When I walk toward an object, I must first want to go there. Second, my feet must take me there. A paralyzed man who wants to walk or an agile man who does not want to walk will both remain where they are. The body politic has the same moving causes. The same distinction can be made between force and will, the latter under the name *legislative power* and the former under the name *executive power*. Nothing is done or at least ought to be done without their concurrence.

We have seen that legislative power belongs to the people and can belong to them alone. On the contrary, it is easy to see by the principles established above that executive power cannot belong to the people at large in its role as legislator or sovereign, since this power consists solely of particular acts that are not within the province of the law, nor consequently of the sovereign, none of whose acts can avoid being laws.

Therefore the public force must have an agent of its own that unifies it and gets it working in accordance with the directions of the general will, that serves as a means of communication between the state and the sovereign, and that accomplishes in the public person just about what the union of soul and body accomplishes in man. This is the reason for having government in the state, something often badly confused with the sovereign, of which it is merely the servant.

What then is the government? An intermediate body established between the subjects and the sovereign for their mutual communication and charged with the execution of the laws and the preservation of liberty, both civil and political.

The members of this body are called magistrates or *kings*, that is to say, *governors*, and the entire body bears the name *prince*.[1] Therefore, those who claim that the act by which a people submit themselves to leaders is not a contract are quite correct. It is absolutely nothing but a commission, an employment in which the leaders, as simple officials of the sovereign, exercise in its own name the power with which it has entrusted them. The sovereign can limit, modify, or reappropriate this power as it pleases, since the alienation of such a right is incompatible with the nature of the social body and contrary to the purpose of the association.

Therefore, I call *government* or supreme administration the legitimate exercise of executive power; I call *prince* or *magistrate* the man or the body charged with that administration.

In government one finds the intermediate forces whose relationships make up that of the whole to the whole or of the sovereign to the state. This last relationship can be represented as one between the extremes of a continuous proportion, whose proportional mean is the government.[2] The government receives from the sovereign the orders it gives the people, and for the state to be in good equilibrium, there must, all things considered, be an equality between the output or the power of the government, taken by itself, and the output or power of the citizens, who are sovereigns on the one hand and subjects on the other.

Moreover, none of these three terms could be altered without the simultaneous destruction of the proportion. If the sovereign wishes to govern, or if the magistrate wishes to give laws, or if the subjects refuse to obey, disorder replaces rule, force and will no longer act in concert, and thus the state dissolves and falls into despotism or anarchy. Finally, since there is only one proportional mean between each relationship, there is only one good government possible for a state. But since a thousand events can change the

---

1. Thus in Venice the college is given the name *Most Serene Prince* even when the doge is not present.
2. [In the language of eighteenth-century mathematics, a continuous proportion is one in which there are two ratios, but the second term of the first is identical to the first term of the second. Thus, if we have sovereign : government and government : state, we have a continuous proportion whose proportional mean is the government and whose extremes are sovereign and state.]

relationships of a people, different governments can be good not only for different peoples but also for the same people at different times.

In trying to provide an idea of the various relationships that can obtain between these two extremes, I will take as an example the number of people, since it is a more easily expressed relationship.

Suppose the state is composed of ten thousand citizens. The sovereign can only be considered collectively and as a body. But each private individual in his position as a subject is regarded as an individual. Thus the sovereign is to the subject as ten thousand is to one. In other words, each member of the state has as his share only one ten-thousandth of the sovereign authority, even though he is totally in subjection to it. If the people are made up of a hundred thousand men, the condition of the subjects does not change, and each bears equally the entire dominion of the laws, while his vote, reduced to one hundred-thousandth, has ten times less influence in the drafting of them. In that case, since the subject always remains one, the ratio of the sovereign to the subject increases in proportion to the number of citizens. Whence it follows that the larger the state becomes, the less liberty there is.

When I say that the ratio increases, I mean that it diverges from equality. Thus the greater the ratio is in the sense employed by geometricians, the less relationship there is in the everyday sense of the word. In the former sense, the ratio, seen in terms of quantity, is measured by the quotient;[3] in the latter sense, the ratio, seen in terms of identity, is reckoned by similarity.

Now the less relationship there is between private wills and the general will, that is, between mores and the laws, the more repressive force ought to increase. Therefore, in order to be good, the government must be relatively stronger in proportion as the people are more numerous.

On the other hand, as the growth of the state gives the trustees of the public authority more temptations and the means of abusing their power, the greater the force the government must have in order to contain the people, the greater the force the sovereign must have in its turn in order to contain the government. I am speaking here not of an absolute force but of the relative force of the various parts of the state.

It follows from this twofold relationship that the continuous proportion between the sovereign, the prince, and the people is in no way an arbitrary idea, but a necessary consequence of the nature of the body politic. It also follows that since one of the extremes, namely, the people as subject, is fixed and represented by unity, whenever the doubled ratio increases or decreases,

---

3. [The quotient here is the second term of a ratio divided by the first. Thus in the ratio 2 : 8, the quotient is 4.]

the simple ratio increases or decreases in like fashion, and that as a consequence the middle term is changed.[4] This makes it clear that there is no unique and absolute constitution of government but that there can be as many governments of differing natures as there are states of differing sizes.

If, in ridiculing this system, someone were to say that in order to find this proportional mean and to form the body of the government, it is necessary merely, in my opinion, to derive the square root of the number of people, I would reply that here I am taking this number only as an example; that the relationships I am speaking of are not measured solely by the number of men but in general by the quantity of action, which is the combination of a multitude of causes; and that, in addition, if to express myself in fewer words I borrow for the moment the terminology of geometry, I nevertheless am not unaware of the fact that geometrical precision has no place in moral quantities.

The government is on a small scale what the body politic that contains it is on a large scale. It is a moral person endowed with certain faculties, active like the sovereign and passive like the state, and capable of being broken down into other similar relationships whence there arises as a consequence a new proportion and yet again another within this one according to the order of tribunals, until an indivisible middle term is reached, that is, a single leader or supreme magistrate, who can be represented in the midst of this progression as the unity between the series of fractions and that of whole numbers.

Without involving ourselves in this multiplication of terms, let us content ourselves with considering the government as a new body in the state, distinct from the people and sovereign and intermediate between them.

The essential difference between these two bodies is that the state exists by itself while the government exists only through the sovereign. Thus the dominant will of the prince is not or should not be anything other than the general will or the law. His force is merely the public force concentrated in him. As soon as he wants to derive from himself some absolute and independent act, the bond that links everything together begins to come loose. If it should finally happen that the prince had a private will more active than that of the sovereign and that he had made use of some of the public force that is available to him in order to obey this private will, so that there would be, so to

---

4. [Take the continuous proportion 8 : 2 and 2 : 4. The doubled ratio, in the language of the time, is (8 × 2) divided by (2 × 4). If the ratios were 4 : 2 and 2 : 1, the doubled ratio would be (4 × 2) divided by 2, i.e., 4; that is, it would be the same as the first term. Moreover, the first term would be the square of the middle terms.]

speak, two sovereigns—one de jure and the other de facto—at that moment the social union would vanish and the body politic would be dissolved.

However, for the body of the government to have an existence, a real life that distinguishes it from the body of the state, and for all its members to be able to act in concert and to fulfill the purpose for which it is instituted, there must be a particular *self*, a sensibility common to all its members, a force or will of its own that tends toward its preservation.

This particular existence presupposes assemblies, councils, a power to deliberate and decide, rights, titles, and privileges that belong exclusively to the prince and that render the condition of the magistrate more honorable in proportion as it is more onerous. The difficulties lie in the manner in which this subordinate whole is so organized within the whole that it in no way alters the general constitution by strengthening its own, that it always distinguishes its particular force, which is intended for its own preservation, from the public force intended for the preservation of the state, and that, in a word, it is always ready to sacrifice the government to the people and not the people to the government.

In addition, although the artificial body of the government is the work of another artificial body and has, in a sense, only a borrowed and subordinate life, this does not prevent it from being capable of acting with more or less vigor or speed or from enjoying, so to speak, more or less robust health. Finally, without departing directly from the purpose of its institution, it can deviate more or less from it, according to the manner in which it is constituted.

From all these differences arise the diverse relationships that the government should have with the body of the state, according to the accidental and particular relationships by which the state itself is modified. For often the government that is best in itself will become the most vicious if its relationships are not altered according to the defects of the body politic to which it belongs.

Chapter 2

On the Principle That Constitutes the Various Forms of Government

In order to lay out the general cause of these differences, a distinction must be made here between the prince and the government, just as I distinguished earlier between the state and the sovereign.

The body of the magistrates can be made up of a larger or smaller number of members. We have said that the ratio of the sovereign to the subjects was greater in proportion as the people were more numerous, and by a manifest analogy we can say the same thing about the government in relation to the magistrates.

Since the total force of the government is always that of the state, it does not vary. Whence it follows that the more of this force it uses on its own members, the less that is left to it for acting on the whole people.

Therefore, the more numerous the magistrates, the weaker the government. Since this maxim is fundamental, let us attempt to explain it more clearly.

We can distinguish in the person of the magistrate three essentially different wills. First, the individual's own will, which tends only to its own advantage. Second, the common will of the magistrates, which is uniquely related to the advantage of the prince. This latter can be called the corporate will and is general in relation to the government and particular in relation to the state, of which the government forms a part. Third, the will of the people or the sovereign will, which is general both in relation to the state considered as the whole and in relation to the government considered as a part of the whole.

In a perfect act of legislation, the private or individual will should be nonexistent; the corporate will proper to the government should be very subordinate; and consequently the general or sovereign will should always be dominant and the unique rule of all the others.

According to the natural order, on the contrary, these various wills become more active in proportion as they are the more concentrated. Thus the general will is always the weakest, the corporate will has second place, and the private will is first of all, so that in the government each member is first himself, then a magistrate, and then a citizen—a gradation directly opposite to the one required by the social order.

Granting this, let us suppose the entire government is in the hands of one single man. In that case the private will and the corporate will are perfectly united, and consequently the latter is at the highest degree of intensity it can reach. But since the use of force is dependent upon the degree of will, and since the absolute force of the government does not vary one bit, it follows that the most active of governments is that of one single man.

On the contrary, let us suppose we are uniting the government to the legislative authority. Let us make the sovereign the prince and all the citizens that many magistrates. Then the corporate will, confused with the general will, will have no more activity than the latter, and will leave the private will all its force. Thus the government, always with the same absolute force, will have its *minimum* relative force or activity.

These relationships are incontestable, and there are still other considerations that serve to confirm them. We see, for example, that each magistrate is more active in his body than each citizen is in his and consequently, that the private will has much more influence on the acts of the government than on those of the sovereign. For each magistrate is nearly always charged with the responsibility for some function of government whereas each citizen, taken by himself, exercises no function of sovereignty. Moreover, the more the state is extended, the more its real force increases, although it does not increase in proportion to its size. But if the state remains the same, the magistrates may be multiplied as much as one likes without the government acquiring any greater real force, since this force is that of the state, whose dimensions [as we have just stipulated] remain the same. Thus the relative force or activity of the government diminishes without its absolute or real force being able to increase.

It is also certain that the execution of public business becomes slower in proportion as more people are charged with the responsibility for it, that in attaching too much importance to prudence, too little importance is attached to fortune, opportunities are missed, and the fruits of deliberation are often lost by dint of deliberation.

I have just proved that the government becomes slack in proportion as the magistrates are multiplied; and I have previously proved that the more numerous the people, the greater should be the increase of repressive force. Whence it follows that the ratio of the magistrate to the government should be the inverse of the ratio of the subjects to the sovereign; that is to say, the more the state increases in size, the more the government should shrink, so that the number of leaders decreases in proportion to the increase in the number of people.

I should add that I am speaking here only about the relative force of the government and not about its rectitude. For, on the contrary, the more numerous the magistrates, the more closely the corporate will approaches the general will, whereas under a single magistrate, the same corporate will is, as I have said, merely a particular will. Thus what can be gained on the one hand is lost on the other, and the art of the legislator is to know how to determine the point at which the government's will and force, always in a reciprocal proportion, are combined in the relationship that is most advantageous to the state.

Chapter 3

Classification of Governments

We have seen in the previous chapter why the various kinds or forms of government are distinguished by the number of members that compose them. It remains to be seen in this chapter how this classification is made.

In the first place, the sovereign can entrust the government to the entire people or to the majority of the people, so that there are more citizens who are magistrates than who are ordinary private citizens. This form of government is given the name *democracy*.

Or else it can restrict the government to the hands of a small number, so that there are more ordinary citizens than magistrates, and this form is called *aristocracy*.

Finally, it can concentrate the entire government in the hands of a single magistrate from whom all the others derive their power. This third form is the most common and is called *monarchy* or royal government.

It should be noted that all these forms, or at least the first two, can be had in greater or lesser degrees and even have a rather wide range. For democracy can include the entire people or be restricted to half. Aristocracy, for its part, can be indeterminately restricted from half the people down to the smallest number. Even royalty can be had in varying levels of distribution. Sparta always had two kings, as required by its constitution; and the Roman Empire is known to have had up to eight emperors at a time, without it being possible to say that the empire was divided. Thus there is a point at which each form of government is indistinguishable from the next, and it is apparent that, under just three names, government can take on as many diverse forms as the state has citizens.

Moreover, since this same government can, in certain respects, be subdivided into other parts, one administered in one way, another in another, there can result from the combination of these three forms a multitude of mixed forms, each of which can be multiplied by all the simple forms.

There has always been a great deal of argument over the best form of government without considering that each one of them is best in certain cases and the worst in others.

If the number of supreme magistrates in the different states ought to be in inverse ratio to that of the citizens, it follows that in general democratic government is suited to small states, aristocratic government to states of intermediate size, and monarchical government to large ones. This rule is derived immediately from the principle; but how is one to count the multitude of circumstances that can furnish exceptions?

Chapter 4
On Democracy

He who makes the law knows better than anyone else how it should be executed and interpreted. It seems therefore to be impossible to have a better constitution than one in which the executive power is united to the legislative power. But this is precisely what renders such a government inadequate in certain respects, since things that should be distinguished are not, and the prince and sovereign, being merely the same person, form, as it were, only a government without a government.

It is not good for the one who makes the laws to execute them, nor for the body of the people to turn its attention away from general perspectives in order to give it[5] to particular objects. Nothing is more dangerous than the influence of private interests on public affairs; and the abuse of the laws by the government is a lesser evil than the corruption of the legislator, which is the inevitable outcome of particular perspectives. In such a situation, since the state has been altered in its essence, all reform becomes impossible. A people that would never misuse the government would never misuse independence. A people that would always govern well would not need to be governed.

Taking the term in the strict sense, a true democracy has never existed and never will. It is contrary to the natural order that the majority governs and the minority is governed. It is unimaginable that the people would remain constantly assembled to handle public affairs, and it is readily apparent that they could not establish commissions for this purpose without changing the form of administration.

In fact, I believe I can lay down as a principle that when the functions of the government are shared among several tribunals, those with the fewest members sooner or later acquire the greatest authority, if only because of the facility in expediting public business that brings this about naturally.

---

5. [Following most modern editions in assuming that Rousseau's *les donner* is a mistake for *la donner*.]

Besides, how many things that are difficult to unite are presupposed by this government? First, a very small state where it is easy for the people to gather together and where each citizen can easily know all the others. Second, a great simplicity of mores, which is an obstacle to the proliferation of public business and thorny discussions. Next, a high degree of equality in ranks and fortunes, without which equality in rights and authority cannot subsist for long. Finally, little or no luxury, for luxury either is the effect of wealth or makes wealth necessary. It simultaneously corrupts both the rich and the poor, the one by possession, the other by covetousness. It sells the homeland to softness and vanity. It takes all its citizens from the state in order to make them slaves to one another, and all of them to opinion.

This is why a famous author[6] has made virtue the principle of the republic. For all these conditions could not subsist without virtue. But owing to his failure to have made the necessary distinctions, this great genius often lacked precision and sometimes clarity. And he did not realize that since the sovereign authority is everywhere the same, the same principle should have a place in every well-constituted state, though in a greater or lesser degree, it is true, according to the form of government.

Let us add that no government is so subject to civil wars and internal agitations as a democratic or popular one, since there is none that tends so forcefully and continuously to change its form or that demands greater vigilance and courage if it is to be maintained in its own form. Above all, it is under this constitution that the citizen ought to arm himself with force and constancy and to say each day of his life from the bottom of his heart what a virtuous Palatine[7] said in the Diet of Poland: *Better to have liberty fraught with danger than servitude in peace.*

Were there a people of gods, it would govern itself democratically. So perfect a government is not suited to men.

---

6. [Montesquieu, *Spirit of the Laws*, bk. 3, ch. 3.]

7. The Palatine of Posen, father of the King of Poland, Duke of Lorraine. [Rousseau quotes in Latin the maxim that follows.]

Chapter 5

On Aristocracy

We have here two very distinct moral persons, namely, the government and the sovereign, and consequently two general wills, one in relation to all the citizens, the other only for the members of the administration. Thus, although the government can regulate its internal administration as it chooses, it can never speak to the people except in the name of the sovereign, that is to say, in the name of the people themselves. This is something never to be forgotten.

The first societies governed themselves aristocratically. The leaders of families deliberated among themselves about public affairs. Young people deferred without difficulty to the authority of experience. This is the origin of the words *priests*, *ancients*, *senate*, and *elders*. The savages of North America still govern themselves that way to this day and are very well governed.

But to the extent that inequality occasioned by social institutions came to prevail over natural inequality, wealth or power[8] was preferred to age, and aristocracy became elective. Finally, the transmission of the father's power, together with his goods, to his children created patrician families; the government was made hereditary, and we find senators who are only twenty years old.

There are therefore three sorts of aristocracy: natural, elective, and hereditary. The first is suited only to simple people; the third is the worst of any government. The second is the best; it is aristocracy properly so called.

In addition to the advantage of the distinction between the two powers, aristocracy has that of the choice of its members. For in popular government all the citizens are born magistrates; however, this type of government limits them to a small number, and they become magistrates only through election,[9] a means by which probity, enlightenment, experience, and all the

---

8. It is clear that among the ancients the word *optimates* does not mean the best but the most powerful.

9. It is of great importance that laws should regulate the form of the election of magistrates, for if it is left to the will of the prince, it is impossible to avoid falling into a hereditary aristocracy, as has taken place in the republics of Venice and Berne. Thus the former has long been a state in dissolution, while the latter maintains itself through the extreme wisdom of its senate. It is a very honorable and very dangerous exception.

other reasons for public preference and esteem are so many new guarantees of being well governed.

Furthermore, assemblies are more conveniently held, public business better discussed and carried out with more orderliness and diligence, the reputation of the state is better sustained abroad by venerable senators than by a multitude that is unknown or despised.

In a word, it is the best and most natural order for the wisest to govern the multitude, provided it is certain that they will govern for its profit and not for their own. There is no need for multiplying devices uselessly or for doing with twenty thousand men what one hundred handpicked men can do even better. But it must be noted here that the corporate interest begins to direct the public force in less strict a conformity with the rule of the general will and that another inevitable tendency removes from the laws a part of the executive power.

With regard to the circumstances that are specifically suitable, a state must not be so small nor its people so simple and upright that the execution of the laws follows immediately from the public will, as is the case in a good democracy. Nor must a nation be so large that the leaders, scattered about in order to govern it, can each play the sovereign in his own department and begin by making themselves independent in order finally to become the masters.

But if aristocracy requires somewhat fewer virtues than popular government, it also demands others that are proper to it, such as moderation among the wealthy and contentment among the poor. For it appears that rigorous equality would be out of place here. It was not observed even in Sparta.

Moreover, if this form of government carries with it a certain inequality of wealth, this is simply in order that in general the administration of public business may be entrusted to those who are best able to give all their time to it, but not, as Aristotle claims,[10] in order that the rich may always be given preference. On the contrary, it is important that an opposite choice should occasionally teach the people that more important reasons for preference are to be found in a man's merit than in his wealth.

---

10. [Rousseau is perhaps interpreting Aristotle, *Politics* bk. 3, ch. 3 (1278a), which maintains that a wealthy artisan can hold office in an oligarchy, but not in an aristocracy, where only the leisured may rule.]

Chapter 6

On Monarchy

So far, we have considered the prince as a moral and collective person, united by the force of laws, and as the trustee of the executive power in the state. We have now to consider this power when it is joined together in the hands of a natural person, of a real man, who alone has the right to dispose of it in accordance with the laws. Such a person is called a monarch or a king.

In utter contrast to the other forms of administration where a collective entity represents an individual, in this form of administration an individual represents a collective entity, so that the moral unity constituting the prince is at the same time a physical unity in which all the faculties that are combined by the law in the other forms of administration with such difficulty are found naturally combined.

Thus the will of the people, the will of the prince, the public force of the state, and the particular force of the government all respond to the same moving agent; all the controls of the machine are in the same hand; everything moves toward the same end; there are no opposing movements that are at cross-purposes with one another; and no constitution is imaginable in which a lesser effort produces a more considerable action. Archimedes sitting serenely on the shore and effortlessly pulling a huge vessel through the waves is what comes to mind when I think of a capable monarch governing his vast states from his private study and making everything move while appearing himself to be immovable.

But if there is no government that has more vigor, there is none where the private will has greater sway and more easily dominates the others. Everything moves toward the same end, it is true; but this end is not that of public felicity, and the very force of the administration unceasingly operates to the detriment of the state.[11]

Kings want to be absolute, and from a distance one cries out to them that the best way to be so is to make themselves loved by their peoples. This maxim is very noble and even very true in certain respects. Unfortunately, it will always be an object of derision in courts. The power that comes from the peoples' love is undoubtedly the greatest, but it is precarious and

---

11. [Although Rousseau recognized monarchy as being, in principle, a legitimate form of government, this and the next paragraph make clear his profound opposition to it. One may conclude that Rousseau was, in some measure, following Machiavelli's example and hiding his love of liberty.]

conditional. Princes will never be satisfied with it. The best kings want to be able to be wicked if it pleases them, without ceasing to be the masters. A political sermonizer might well say to them that since the people's force is their force, their greatest interest is that the people should be flourishing, numerous, and formidable. They know perfectly well that this is not true. Their personal interest is first of all that the people should be weak and miserable and incapable of ever resisting them. I admit that, assuming the subjects were always in perfect submission, the interest of the prince would then be for the people to be powerful, so that this power, being his own, would render him formidable in the eyes of his neighbors. But since this interest is merely secondary and subordinate, and since the two assumptions are incompatible, it is natural that the princes should always give preference to the maxim that is the most immediately useful to them. This is the point that Samuel made so forcefully to the Hebrews and that Machiavelli has made apparent. Under the pretext of teaching kings, he has taught important lessons to the peoples. Machiavelli's *The Prince* is the book for republicans.[12]

We have found, through general relationships, that the monarchy is suited only to large states, and we find this again in examining the monarchy itself. The more numerous the public administration, the more the ratio of the prince to subjects diminishes and approaches equality, so that this ratio is one or equality itself in a democracy. This same ratio increases in proportion as the government is restricted, and is at its *maximum* when the government is in the hands of a single man. Then there is too great a distance between the prince and the people, and the state lacks cohesiveness. In order to bring about this cohesiveness, there must therefore be intermediate orders;[13] there must be princes, grandees, and a nobility to fill them. Now none of this is suited to a small state, which is ruined by all these social levels.

But if it is difficult for a large state to be well governed, it is much harder still for it to be well governed by just one man, and everyone knows what happens when the king appoints substitutes.

---

12. [The following was inserted in the 1782 edition: "Machiavelli was a decent man and a good citizen. But since he was attached to the house of Medici, he was forced during the oppression of his homeland to disguise his love of liberty. The very choice of his execrable hero makes clear enough his hidden intention. And the contrast between the maxims of his book *The Prince* and those of his *Discourses on Titus Livy* and of his *History of Florence* shows that this profound political theorist has until now had only superficial or corrupt readers. The court of Rome has sternly prohibited his book. I can well believe it; it is the court he most clearly depicts."]

13. [Cf. Montesquieu, *Spirit of the Laws*, bk. 2, ch. 4.]

An essential and inevitable defect, which will always place the monarchical form of government below the republican form, is that in the latter form the public voice hardly ever raises to the highest positions men who are not enlightened and capable and who would not fill their positions with honor.[14] On the contrary, those who attain these positions in monarchies are most often petty bunglers, petty swindlers, petty intriguers, whose petty talents, which cause them to attain high positions at court, serve only to display their incompetence to the public as soon as they reach these positions. The people are much less often in error in their choice than the prince, and a man of real merit in the ministry is almost as rare as a fool at the head of a republican government. Thus, when by some happy chance one of these men who are born to govern takes the helm of public business in a monarchy that has nearly been sunk by this crowd of fine managers, there is utter amazement at the resources he finds, and his arrival marks an era in the history of the country.[15]

For a monarchical state to be capable of being well governed, its size or extent must be proportionate to the faculties of the one who governs. It is easier to conquer than to rule. With a long enough lever it is possible for a single finger to make the world shake; but holding it in place requires the shoulders of Hercules. However small a state may be, the prince is nearly always too small for it. When, on the contrary, it happens that the state is too small for its leader, which is quite rare, it is still poorly governed, since the leader, always pursuing his grand schemes, forgets the interests of the peoples, making them no less wretched through the abuse of talents he has too much of than does a leader who is limited for want of what he lacks. A kingdom must, so to speak, expand or contract with each reign, depending on the ability of the prince. By contrast, since the talents of a senate have a greater degree of stability, the state can have permanent boundaries without the administration working any less well.

The most obvious disadvantage of the government of just one man is the lack of that continuous line of succession that forms an unbroken bond of unity in the other two forms of government. When one king dies, another is needed. Elections leave dangerous intervals and are stormy. And unless

---

14. [Cf. Montesquieu, *Spirit of the Laws*, bk. 2, ch. 2; the same point is made by Machiavelli.]
15. [This sentence was added as the book went through the press (letter to Rey, January 6, 1762) and was intended as praise of the leading minister of the day, Choiseul. Rousseau (mistakenly) hoped it would encourage him to oppose any move to ban the *Social Contract* in France.]

the citizens have a disinterestedness and integrity that seldom accompany this form of government, intrigue and corruption enter the picture. It is difficult for one to whom the state has sold itself not to sell it in turn and reimburse himself at the expense of the weak for the money extorted from him by the powerful. Sooner or later everything becomes venal under such an administration, and then the peace enjoyed under kings is worse than the disorders of the interregna.

What has been done to prevent these ills? Crowns have been made hereditary within certain families, and an order of succession has been established that prevents all dispute when kings die. That is to say, by substituting the disadvantage of regencies for that of elections, an apparent tranquility has been preferred to a wise administration, the risk of having children, monsters, or imbeciles for leaders has been preferred to having to argue over the choice of good kings. No consideration has been given to the fact that in being thus exposed to the risk of the alternative, nearly all the odds are against them. There was a lot of sense in what Dionysius the Younger said in reply to his father, who, while reproaching his son for some shameful action, said, "Have I given you such an example?" "Ah," replied the son, "but your father was not king."

When a man has been elevated to command others, everything conspires to deprive him of justice and reason. A great deal of effort is made, it is said, to teach young princes the art of ruling. It does not appear that this education does them any good. It would be better to begin by teaching them the art of obeying. The greatest kings whom history celebrates were not brought up to reign. It is a science that one is never less in possession of than after one has learned it too much, and that one acquires better by obeying than by commanding. "For the most useful as well as the shortest method of finding out what is good and what is bad is to consider what you would have wished or not wished to have happened under another prince."[16]

One result of this lack of coherence is the instability of the royal form of government, which, now regulated by one plan now by another according to the character of the ruling prince or of those who rule for him, cannot have a fixed objective for very long or a consistent policy. This variation always causes the state to drift from maxim to maxim, from project to project, and does not take place in the other forms of government, where the prince is always the same. It is also apparent that in general, if there is more cunning in a royal court, there is more wisdom in a senate and that republics proceed toward their objectives by means of policies that are more consistent and

---

16. Tacitus, *Histories*, Book I. [Rousseau here quotes the Latin.]

better followed. However, each revolution in the ministry produces a revolution in the state, since the maxim common to all ministers and nearly all kings is to do the reverse of their predecessor in everything. From this same incoherence we derive the solution to a sophism that is very familiar to royalist political theorists. Not only is civil government compared to domestic government and the prince to the father of the family (an error already refuted), but this magistrate is also liberally given all the virtues he might need, and it is always presupposed that the prince is what he ought to be. With the help of this presupposition, the royal form of government is obviously preferable to any other, since it is unquestionably the strongest; and it lacks only a corporate will that is more in conformity with the general will in order to be the best as well.

But if, according to Plato,[17] a king by nature is such a rare person, how many times will nature and fortune converge to crown him; and if a royal education necessarily corrupts those who receive it, what is to be hoped from a series of men who have been brought up to reign? Surely then it is deliberate self-deception to confuse the royal form of government with that of a good king. To see what this form of government is in itself, we need to consider it under princes who are incompetent or wicked, for either they come to the throne wicked or incompetent or else the throne makes them so.

These difficulties have not escaped the attention of our authors, but they have not been troubled by them. The remedy, they say, is to obey without a murmur. God in his anger gives us bad kings, and they must be endured as punishments from heaven. No doubt this sort of talk is edifying; however, I do not know but that it belongs more in a pulpit than in a book on political theory. What is to be said of a physician who promises miracles and whose art consists entirely of exhorting his sick patient to practice patience? It is quite obvious that we must put up with a bad government when that is what we have. The question would be how to find a good one.

---

17. *The Statesman* [301C-E].

Chapter 7

On Mixed Government

Strictly speaking, there is no such thing as a simple form of government. A single leader must have subordinate magistrates; a popular government must have a leader. Thus in the distribution of the executive power there is always a gradation from the greater to the lesser number, with the difference that sometimes the greater number depends on the few, and sometimes the few depend on the greater number.

At times the distribution is equal, either when the constitutive parts are in a state of mutual dependence, as in the government of England, or when the authority of each part is independent but imperfect, as in Poland.[18] This latter form is bad, since there is no unity in the government and the state lacks a bond of unity.

Which one is better, a simple or a mixed form of government? A question much debated among political theorists, to which the same reply must be given that I gave above regarding every form of government.

In itself the simple form of government is the best, precisely because it is simple. But when the executive power is not sufficiently dependent upon the legislative power, that is to say, when there is a closer relationship between the prince and the sovereign than there is between the people and the prince, this defect in the proportion must be remedied by dividing the government; for then all of its parts have no less authority over the subjects, and their division makes all of them together less forceful against the sovereign.

The same disadvantage can also be prevented through the establishment of intermediate magistrates, who, by being utterly separate from the government, serve merely to balance the two powers and to maintain their respective rights. In that case, the government is not mixed; it is tempered.

The opposite difficulty can be remedied by similar means. Thus when the government is too slack, tribunals can be set up to give it a concentrated focus. This is done in all democracies. In the first case the government is divided in order to weaken it, and in the second to strengthen it. For the *maximum* of force and weakness are both found in the simple forms of

---

18. [Rousseau has in mind Montesquieu's account of the English constitution; in Poland (or at least so Rousseau believed) ministers were in effect unaccountable and could do as they pleased.]

government, while the mixed forms of government provide an intermediate amount of strength.

Chapter 8

That Not All Forms of Government Are Suited to All Countries

Since liberty is not a fruit of every climate, it is not within the reach of all peoples. The more one meditates on this principle established by Montesquieu,[19] the more one is aware of its truth. The more one contests it, the more occasions there are for establishing it by means of new proofs.

In all the governments in the world, the public person consumes but produces nothing. Whence therefore does it get the substance it consumes? It is from the labor of its members. It is the surplus of private individuals that produces what is needed by the public. Whence it follows that the civil state can subsist only as long as men's labor produces more than they need.

Now this surplus is not the same in every country in the world. In many countries it is considerable; in others it is moderate; in others it is nil; in still others it is negative.

This ratio depends on the fertility of the climate, the sort of labor the land requires, the nature of its products, the force of its inhabitants, the greater or lesser consumption they need, and many other similar ratios of which it is composed.

On the other hand, not all governments are of the same nature. They are more or less voracious; and the differences are founded on this added principle that the greater the distance the public contributions have to travel from their source, the more onerous they are. It is not on the basis of the amount of the taxes that this burden is to be measured, but on the basis of the path they have to travel in order to return to the hands from which they came. When this circulation is prompt and well established, it is unimportant whether one pays little or a great deal. The people are always rich and the finances are always in good shape. On the contrary, however little the people give, when this small amount does not return, it is soon wiped out by continual giving. The state is never rich and the people are always destitute.

---

19. [Montesquieu, *Spirit of the Laws*, especially bk. 17.]

It follows from this that the greater the distance between the people and the government, the more onerous the taxes become. Thus in a democracy the people are the least burdened; in an aristocracy they are more so; in a monarchy they bear the heaviest weight. Monarchy, therefore, is suited only to wealthy nations; aristocracy to states of moderate wealth and size; democracy to states that are small and poor.

In fact, the more one reflects on it, the more one finds in this the difference between free and monarchical states. In the former, everything is used for the common utility. In the latter, the public and private forces are reciprocal, the one being augmented by the weakening of the other. Finally, instead of governing subjects in order to make them happy, despotism makes them miserable in order to govern them.

Thus in each climate there are natural causes on the basis of which one can assign the form of government that the force of the climate requires and can even say what kind of inhabitants it should have. Barren and unproductive lands, where the product is not worth the labor, ought to remain uncultivated and deserted or peopled only by savages. Places where men's labor yields only what is necessary ought to be inhabited by barbarous peoples; in places such as these, all polity[20] would be impossible. Places where the surplus of products over labor is moderate are suited to free peoples. Those where an abundant and fertile soil produces a great deal in return for a small amount of labor require a monarchical form of government, in order that the subject's excess of surplus may be consumed by the prince's luxurious living. For it is better for this excess to be absorbed by the government than dissipated by private individuals. I realize that there are exceptions; but these exceptions themselves prove the rule, in that sooner or later they produce revolutions that restore things to the order of nature.

General laws should always be distinguished from the particular causes that can modify their effect. Even if the entire south were covered with republics and the entire north with despotic states, it would still be no less true that the effect of climate makes despotism suited to hot countries, barbarism to cold countries, and good polity to intermediate regions. I also realize that, while granting the principle, disputes may arise over its application. It could be said that there are cold countries that are very fertile and southern ones that are quite barren. But this poses a difficulty only for those

---

20. [Rousseau's word is *politie*, which does not appear in eighteenth-century French dictionaries and would therefore have been more unusual than "polity." He means "political community."]

who have not examined the thing in all its relationships. As I have said, it is necessary to take into account those of labor, force, consumption, and so on. Let us suppose that there are two parcels of land of equal size, one of which yields five units and the other ten. If the inhabitants of the first parcel consume four units and the inhabitants of the second consume nine, the excess of the first will be one-fifth and that of the other will be one-tenth. Since the ratio of these two excesses is therefore the inverse of that of the products, the parcel of land that produces only five units will yield a surplus that is double that of the parcel of land that produces ten.

But it is not a question of a doubled product, and I do not believe that anyone dares, as a general rule, to place the fertility of a cold country even on an equal footing with that of hot countries. Nevertheless, let us assume that this equality is the case. Let us, if you will, reckon England to be the equal of Sicily, and Poland the equal of Egypt. Further south we have Africa and the Indies; further north we have nothing at all. To achieve this equality of product, what difference must there be in agricultural techniques? In Sicily one needs merely to scratch the soil; in England what efforts it demands to work it! Now where more hands are needed to obtain the same product, the surplus must necessarily be less.

Consider too that the same number of men consumes much less in hot countries. The climate demands that a person keep sober in order to be in good health. Europeans wanting to live there just as they do at home would all die of dysentery and indigestion. "We are," says Chardin, "carnivorous beasts, wolves, in comparison with the Asians. Some attribute the sobriety of the Persians to the fact that their land is less cultivated. On the contrary, I believe that this country is less abundant in commodities because the inhabitants need less. If their frugality," he continues, "were an effect of the country's scarcity, only the poor would eat little; however, it is generally the case that everyone does so. And more or less would be eaten in each province according to the fertility of the country; however, the same sobriety is found throughout the kingdom. They take great pride in their lifestyle, saying that one has only to look at their complexions to recognize how far it excels that of the Christians. In fact, the complexion of the Persians is clear. They have fair skin, fine and polished, whereas the complexion of their Armenian subjects, who live in the European style, is coarse and blotchy, and their bodies are fat and heavy."[21]

21. [Jean Chardin (1643–1713), *Voyages en Perse*, 4 vols. (Amsterdam, 1735), vol. 3, 76, 83–84. The first edition is 1711.]

The closer you come to the equator, the less people live on. They rarely eat meat; rice, maize, couscous, millet, and cassava are their usual diet. In the Indies there are millions of men whose sustenance costs less than a penny a day. In Europe itself we see noticeable differences in appetite between the peoples of the north and the south. A Spaniard will live for eight days on a German's dinner. In countries where men are the most voracious, luxury too turns toward things edible. In England, luxury is shown in a table loaded with meats; in Italy you are regaled with sugar and flowers.

Luxury in clothing also offers similar differences. In the climate where the seasonal changes are sudden and violent, people have better and simpler clothing. In climates where people clothe themselves merely for ornamental purposes, flashiness is more sought after than utility. The clothes themselves are a luxury there. In Naples you see men strolling every day along the Posilippo decked out in gold-embroidered coats and bare legged. It is the same with buildings; magnificence is the sole consideration when there is nothing to fear from the weather. In Paris or London, people want to be housed warmly and comfortably. In Madrid, there are superb salons, but no windows that close, and people sleep in rat holes.

In hot countries foodstuffs are considerably more substantial and succulent. This is a third difference that cannot help but influence the second. Why do people eat so many vegetables in Italy? Because there they are good, nourishing, and have an excellent flavor. In France, where vegetables are fed nothing but water, they are not nourishing at all and are nearly counted for nothing at table. Be that as it may, they occupy no less land and cost at least as much effort to cultivate. It is a known fact that the wheats of Barbary, in other respects inferior to those of France, yield far more flour, and that those of France, for their part, yield more flour than those of the north. It can be inferred from this that a similar gradation in the same direction is generally observed from the equator to the pole. Now is it not a distinct disadvantage to have a smaller quantity of nourishment from equal amounts of produce?

To all these different considerations, I can add one that depends on and strengthens them. It is that hot countries have less of a need for inhabitants than do cold countries and yet could feed more of them. This produces a double surplus, always to the advantage of despotism. The greater the area occupied by the same number of inhabitants, the more difficult it becomes to revolt, since concerted action cannot be taken promptly and secretly; and it is always easy for the government to discover plots and cut off communications. But the closer together a numerous people are drawn, the less the government can usurp from the sovereign. The leaders deliberate as safely in their rooms as the prince does in his council, and the crowd assembles as quickly in public squares as do troops in their barracks. In this regard, it is to the advantage of a tyrannical government, therefore, to act over great distances. With the help of the points of support it establishes, its force increases with distance like that of levers.[22] On the contrary, the strength of the people acts only when concentrated; it evaporates and is lost as it spreads, like the effect of gunpowder scattered on the ground, which catches fire only one grain at a time. The least populated countries are thus the best suited for tyranny. Ferocious animals reign only in deserts.

Chapter 9

On the Signs[23] *of a Good Government*

When the question arises which one is absolutely the best government, an insoluble question is being raised because it is indeterminate. Or, if you wish, it has as many good answers as there are possible combinations in the absolute and relative positions of peoples.

But if it is asked by what sign it is possible to know that a given people are well or poorly governed, this is another matter, and the question of fact could be resolved.

---

22. This does not contradict what I said earlier in Book II, Chapter 9, regarding the disadvantages of large states, for there it was a question of the authority of the government over its members, and here it is a question of its force against the subjects. Its scattered members serve it as points of support for acting from a distance upon the people, but it has no support for acting directly on these members themselves. Thus in the one case the length of the lever causes its weakness, and in the other case its force. [This note was added as the *Social Contract* was on its way through the press: letter to Rey, February 18, 1762.]

23. [The word *signe* (sign) is used in early modern French to refer to something that is an indication of something else; thus, a high temperature indicates a fever, and the tracks left by a wolf indicate its presence nearby. Rousseau would also have had available the words *symptome* and *indice*. The French language still lacks a word equivalent to "evidence" (in the sense that we describe a legal case as being based on "evidence." The French speak of testimony, proofs, and indications [*indices*] where we have one word that covers all three). Rousseau's word *signe* thus means something close to "evidence," but the term "evidence" carries with it the values and procedures of modern science, and it would, arguably, be anachronistic to ascribe these to Rousseau.]

However, there is no answer forthcoming, since each wants to answer it in his own way. The subjects praise public tranquility; the citizens praise the liberty of private individuals. The former prefers the security of possessions; the latter that of persons. The former has it that the best government is the one that is most severe; the latter maintains that the best government is the one that is mildest. This one wants crimes to be punished, and that one wants them prevented. The former think it a good thing to be feared by their neighbors; the latter prefer to be ignored by them. The one is content as long as money circulates; the other demands that the people have bread. Even if agreement were had on these and similar points, would we be any closer to an answer? Since moral quantities do not allow of precise measurement, even if there were agreement regarding the index, how could there be agreement regarding the evaluation?

For my part, I am always astonished that a sign that is straightforward is overlooked or that people are of such bad faith as not to agree on it. What is the goal of the political association? It is the preservation and prosperity of its members. And what is the surest sign that they are preserved and prospering? It is their number and their population. Therefore, do not go looking elsewhere for this much disputed sign. All other things being equal, the government under which, without external means, without naturalizations, without colonies, the citizens become populous and multiply the most is infallibly the best government. That government under which a people diminish and die out is the worst. Statisticians, it is now up to you. Count, measure, compare.[24]

---

24. [This note was added while the *Social Contract* was on its way through the press: letter to Rey, February 18, 1762.] We should judge on this same principle the centuries that merit preference with respect to the prosperity of the human race. Those in which letters and arts are known to have flourished have been admired too much, without penetrating the secret object of their cultivation and without considering its devastating effect, "and this was called humanity by the inexperienced, when it was a part of servitude." [Rousseau here quotes Tacitus, *Agricola*, ch. 21, in Latin.] Will we never see in the maxims of books the crude interest that causes the authors to speak? No. Whatever they may say, when a country is depopulated, it is not true, despite its brilliance, that all goes well; and the fact that a poet has an income of a hundred thousand livres is not sufficient to make his century the best of all. The apparent calm and the tranquility of the leader ought to be less of an object of consideration than the well-being of whole nations and especially of the most populous states. A hailstorm may devastate a few cantons, but it rarely causes famine. Riots and civil wars may greatly disturb the leaders, but they are not the true misfortunes of the people, who may even have a reprieve while people argue over who will tyrannize them. It is their permanent condition that causes real periods of prosperity

Chapter 10

On the Abuse of Government and Its Tendency to Degenerate

Just as the private will acts constantly against the general will, so the government makes a continual effort against sovereignty. The more this effort increases, the more the constitution is altered. And since there is here no other corporate will that, by resisting the will of the prince, would create an equilibrium with it, sooner or later the prince must finally oppress the sovereign and break the social treaty. That is the inherent and inevitable vice that, from the birth of the body politic, tends unceasingly to destroy it, just as old age and death destroy the human body.

There are two general ways in which a government degenerates, namely when it shrinks or when the state dissolves.

The government shrinks when it passes from a large to a small number, that is to say, from democracy to aristocracy and from aristocracy to royalty. That is its natural inclination.[25] If it were to go backward from a small

---

or calamity. It is when everything remains crushed under the yoke that everything decays. It is then that the leaders destroy them at will, "where they bring about solitude they call it peace." [Rousseau here quotes Tacitus, *Agricola*, ch. 30, in Latin.] When the quarrels of the great disturbed the kingdom of France, and the coadjutor of Paris brought with him to the *parlement* a dagger in his pocket, this did not keep the French people from living happily and in great numbers in a free and decent ease. Long ago, Greece flourished in the midst of the cruelest wars. Blood flowed in waves, and the whole country was covered with men. It seemed, says Machiavelli [Rousseau paraphrases a passage in Machiavelli's *History of Florence*], that in the midst of murders, proscriptions, and civil wars, our republic became more powerful; the virtue of its citizens, their mores, and their independence did more to reinforce it than all its dissensions did to weaken it. A little agitation gives strength to souls, and what truly brings about prosperity for the species is not so much peace as liberty. [In "quarrels of the great disturbed the kingdom of France," Rousseau is referring to the civil war known as the second Fronde, or the Fronde of the nobles, 1650–1653. Rousseau's source is the *Mémoires* of the Cardinal de Retz. De Retz tells this story about himself—with some sense of shame because the clergy (coadjutor, assistant to a bishop) are not meant to carry weapons or shed blood.]
25. The slow formation and the progress of the Republic of Venice in its lagoons offers a notable example of this succession. And it is rather astonishing that after more than twelve hundred years the Venetians seem to be no further than the second stage, which began with the *Serrar di Consiglio* in 1198. As for the ancient dukes, for whom the Venetians are reproached, whatever the *Squitinio della libertà veneta* [an

number to a large number, it could be said to slacken, but this backward movement is impossible.

In fact, the government never changes its form except when its exhausted energy leaves it too enfeebled to be capable of preserving what belongs to it. Now if it were to become still more slack while it expanded, its force would become entirely null; it would be still less likely to subsist. It must therefore be wound up and tightened in proportion as it gives way; otherwise the state it sustains would fall into ruin.

The dissolution of the state can come about in two ways.

First, when the prince no longer administers the state in accordance with the laws and usurps the sovereign power. In that case a remarkable change

---

anonymous attack on Venice published in 1612] may say about them, it has been proven that they were not their sovereigns.

The Roman Republic does not fail to be brought forward as an objection against me, which, it will be said, followed a completely opposite course, passing from monarchy to aristocracy to democracy. That is not how I see it at all.

The first establishment of Romulus was a mixed government that promptly degenerated into despotism. For some particular reasons, the state perished before its time, just as one sees a newborn die before reaching manhood. The expulsion of the Tarquins was the true epoch of the birth of the republic. But it did not at first take on a constant form, because in failing to abolish the patriciate, only half the work was completed. For in this way, since hereditary aristocracy, which is the worst of all forms of legitimate administration, remained in conflict with democracy, the form of government remained uncertain and adrift and was not fixed, as Machiavelli has proven [*Discourses*, bk. 1, chs. 2–3], until the establishment of the tribunes. It was only then that there was a true government and a veritable democracy. In fact, the people then were not merely sovereign but also magistrate and judge. The senate was merely a subordinate tribunal whose purpose was to temper and concentrate the government; and the consuls themselves, though they were patricians, the first magistrates, and absolute generals in war, in Rome were merely presiding officers of the people.

From that point on, the government was also seen to follow its natural inclination and to tend strongly toward aristocracy. With the patriciate having abolished itself, as it were, the aristocracy was no longer in the body of patricians, as it is in Venice and Genoa, but in the body of the senate, which was composed of patricians and plebeians, and even in the body of the tribunes when they began to usurp an active power. For words do not affect things, and when the people have leaders who govern for them, it is always an aristocracy, regardless of the name these leaders bear.

The abuse of aristocracy gave birth to civil wars and the triumvirate. Sulla, Julius Caesar, and Augustus became in fact veritable monarchs, and finally, under the despotism of Tiberius, the state was dissolved. Roman history therefore does not invalidate my principle; it confirms it.

takes place, namely that it is not the government but the state that shrinks. I mean that the state as a whole is dissolved, and another is formed inside it, composed exclusively of the members of the government, and that is no longer anything for the rest of the people but their master and tyrant. As a result, the instant that the government usurps sovereignty, the social compact is broken, and all ordinary citizens, on recovering by right their natural liberty, are forced but not obliged to obey.

The same thing happens also when the members of the government separately usurp the power they should only exercise as a body. This is no less an infraction of the laws and produces even greater disorder. Under these circumstances, there are, so to speak, as many princes as magistrates, and the state, no less divided than the government, perishes or changes its form.

When the state dissolves, the abuse of government, whatever it is, takes the common name *anarchy*. To distinguish, democracy degenerates into *ochlocracy*, aristocracy into *oligarchy*. I would add that royalty degenerates into *tyranny*; however, this latter term is equivocal and requires an explanation.

In the ordinary sense, a tyrant is a king who governs with violence and without regard for justice and the laws. In the strict sense, a tyrant is a private individual who arrogates to himself royal authority without having any right to it. This is how the Greeks understood the word *tyrant*. They gave the name indifferently to good and bad princes whose authority was not legitimate.[26] Thus *tyrant* and *usurper* are two perfectly synonymous words.

To give different names to different things, I call the usurper of royal authority a *tyrant*, and the usurper of sovereign power a *despot*. The tyrant is someone who intrudes himself, contrary to the laws, in order to govern according to the laws. The despot is someone who places himself above the laws themselves. Thus the tyrant need not be a despot, but the despot is always a tyrant.

---

26. "For all are considered and are called tyrants who use perpetual power in a city accustomed to liberty." [Rousseau here quotes the Latin.] Cornelius Nepos, *Life of Miltiades*. It is true that Aristotle, *Nicomachean Ethics*, Book VIII, Chapter 10 [1160b], distinguishes between a tyrant and a king, in that the former governs for his own utility and the latter governs only for the utility of his subjects. But besides the fact that generally all the Greek authors used the word *tyrant* in another sense, as appears most clearly in Xenophon's *Hiero*, it would follow from Aristotle's distinction that there has not yet been a single king since the beginning of the world.

Chapter 11

On the Death of the Body Politic

Such is the natural and inevitable tendency of the best-constituted governments. If Sparta and Rome perished, what state can hope to last forever? If we wish to form a durable establishment, let us then not dream of making it eternal. To succeed, one must not attempt the impossible or flatter oneself with giving to the work of men a solidity that things human do not allow.

The body politic, like the human body, begins to die from the very moment of its birth and carries within itself the causes of its destruction. But both can have a constitution that is more or less robust and suited to preserve them for a longer or shorter time. The constitution of man is the work of nature; the constitution of the state is the work of art. It is not within men's power to prolong their lives; it is within their power to prolong the life of the state as far as possible by giving it the best constitution it can have. The best-constituted state will come to an end, but later than another, if no unforeseen accident brings about its premature fall.

The principle of political life is in the sovereign authority. Legislative power is the heart of the state; the executive power is the brain, which gives movement to all the parts. The brain can fall into paralysis and yet the individual may still live. A man may remain an imbecile and live. But once the heart has ceased its functions, the animal is dead.

It is not through laws that the state subsists; it is through legislative power. Yesterday's law does not obligate today, but tacit consent is presumed from silence, and the sovereign is taken to be giving incessant confirmation to the laws it does not abrogate while having the power to do so. Whatever it has once declared it wants it still wants unless it revokes its declaration.

Why then is so much respect paid to ancient laws? For just this very reason. We must believe that nothing but the excellence of the ancient wills could have preserved them for so long. If the sovereign had not constantly recognized them to be salutary, it would have revoked them a thousand times. This is why, far from growing weak, the laws continually acquire new force in every well-constituted state. The prejudice in favor of antiquity each day renders them more venerable. However, wherever the laws weaken as they grow old, this proves that there is no longer a legislative power and that the state is no longer alive.

Chapter 12

How the Sovereign Authority Is Maintained

The sovereign, having no other force than legislative power, acts only through the laws. And since the laws are only authentic acts of the general will, the sovereign can act only when the people are assembled. When the people are assembled, it will be said, what a chimera! It is a chimera today, but two thousand years ago it was not. Have men changed their nature?

The boundaries of what is possible in moral matters are less narrow than we think. It is our weaknesses, our vices, and our prejudices that shrink them. Base souls do not believe in great men; vile slaves smile with an air of mockery at this word *liberty*.

Let us consider what can be done in the light of what has been done. I will not speak of the ancient republics of Greece; however, the Roman Republic was, to my mind, a great state, and the town of Rome was a great town. The last census in Rome gave four hundred thousand citizens bearing arms, and the last census count of the empire gave four million citizens, not counting subjects, foreigners, women, children, and slaves.

What difficulty might not be imagined in frequently calling assemblies of the immense people of that capital and its environs? Nevertheless, few weeks passed by without the Roman people being assembled, and even several times in one week. They exercised not only the rights of sovereignty but also a part of those of the government. They took care of certain matters of public business, they tried certain cases, and this entire people were in the public meeting place hardly less often as magistrates than as citizens.

In looking back to the earliest history of nations, one would find that most of the ancient governments, even the monarchical ones such as those of the Macedonians and the Franks, had similar councils. Be that as it may, this lone incontestable fact answers every difficulty: arguing from the actual to the possible seems like good logic to me.

73

Chapter 13

Continuation

It is not enough for an assembled people to have once determined the constitution of the state by sanctioning a body of laws. It is not enough for them to have established a perpetual government or to have provided once and for all for the election of magistrates. In addition to the extraordinary assemblies that unforeseen situations can necessitate, there must be some fixed, periodic assemblies that nothing can abolish or prorogue, so that on a specified day the people are rightfully convened by law, without the need for any other formal convocation.[27]

But apart from these assemblies that are lawful by their date alone, any assembly of the people that has not been convened by the magistrates appointed for that task and in accordance with the prescribed forms should be regarded as illegitimate, and all that takes place there should be regarded as null, since the order itself to assemble ought to emanate from the law.

As to the question of the greater or lesser frequency of legitimate assemblies, this depends on so many considerations that no precise rules can be given about it. All that can be said is that in general the more force a government has, the more frequently the sovereign ought to show itself.

I will be told that this may be fine for a single town, but what is to be done when the state includes several? Will the sovereign authority be divided, or will it be concentrated in a single town with all the rest made subject to it?

I answer that neither should be done. In the first place, the sovereign authority is simple and one; it cannot be divided without being destroyed. In the second place, a town cannot legitimately be in subjection to another town, any more than a nation can be in subjection to another nation, since the essence of the body politic consists in the harmony of obedience and liberty; and the words *subject* and *sovereign* are identical correlatives, whose meaning is combined in the single word *citizen*.

I answer further that it is always an evil to unite several towns in a single city,[28] and that anyone wanting to bring about this union should not expect

---

27. [In Rousseau's view the absence of such assemblies of the general council was a major weakness of the Genevan constitution, allowing the oligarchical little council to usurp powers that properly belonged to the people as a whole.]
28. [Rousseau's word is *cité*. See note 26 and p. xxxviii of the Introduction for his understanding of the meaning of the word as referring to any political community where there is a common citizenship. Since he took such care to define the word,

to avoid its natural disadvantages. The abuses of large states should not be raised as an objection against someone who wants only small ones. But how are small states to be given enough force to resist the large ones? Just as the Greek cities long ago resisted a great king, and more recently Holland and Switzerland have resisted the house of Austria.

Nevertheless, if the state cannot be reduced to appropriate boundaries, one expedient still remains: not to allow a fixed capital, to make the seat of government move from one town to another, and to assemble the estates of the country in each of them in their turn.

Populate the territory uniformly, extend the same rights everywhere, spread abundance and life all over. In this way the state will become simultaneously as strong and as well governed as possible. Recall that town walls are built completely with materials from the wreckage of rural houses. With each palace I see being erected in the capital, I believe I see an entire countryside reduced to ruins.

Chapter 14

Continuation

Once the people are legitimately assembled as a sovereign body, all jurisdiction of the government ceases, the executive power is suspended, and the person of the humblest citizen is as sacred and inviolable as that of the first magistrate; for where those who are represented are found, there is no longer any representative. Most of the tumults that arose in the comitia in Rome were due to ignorance or neglect of this rule. On such occasions the consuls were merely the presiding officers of the people; the tribunes, ordinary speakers;[29] the senate, nothing at all.

These intervals of suspension, during which the prince recognizes or ought to recognize an actual superior, have always been disturbing for him. And these assemblies of the people, which are the shield of the body politic

---

this translation sticks to it, but his sense might be more easily rendered by "political community" or "polity."]

29. In nearly the same sense as is given this word in the English Parliament. [The speaker presides over debates in the British House of Commons, as in the U.S. House of Representatives.] The similarity between these activities would have put the consuls and the tribunes in conflict, even if all jurisdiction had been suspended.

and the curb on the government, have at all times been the horror of leaders. Thus they never spare efforts, objections, difficulties, or promises to keep the citizens from having them. When the citizens are greedy, cowardly, and pusillanimous, more enamored of repose than of liberty, they do not hold out very long against the redoubled efforts of the government. Thus it is that, as the resisting force constantly grows, the sovereign authority finally vanishes, and the majority of political communities fall and perish prematurely.

But between the sovereign authority and arbitrary government, there sometimes is introduced an intermediate power about which we must speak.

Chapter 15

On Deputies or Representatives

Once public service ceases to be the chief business of the citizens, and they prefer to serve with their wallet rather than with their person, the state is already near its ruin. Is it necessary to march off to battle? They pay mercenary troops and stay at home. Is it necessary to go to the council? They name deputies and stay at home. By dint of laziness and money, they finally have soldiers to enslave the country and representatives to sell it.

The hustle and bustle of commerce and the arts, the avid interest in profits, softness, and the love of amenities: these are what change personal services into money. A person gives up part of his profit in order to increase it at his convenience. Give money and soon you will be in chains. The word *finance* is a slave's word. It is unknown in the city. In a truly free state the citizens do everything with their own hands and nothing with money. Far from paying to be exempted from their duties, they would pay to fulfill them themselves. Far be it from me to be sharing commonly held ideas; I believe that forced labor is less opposed to liberty than are taxes.

The better a state is constituted, the more public business takes precedence over private business in the minds of the citizens. There even is far less private business since, with the sum of common happiness providing a more considerable portion of each individual's happiness, less remains for him to look for through private efforts. In a well-run city everyone flies to the assemblies; under a bad government no one wants to take a step to get to them, since no one takes an interest in what happens there, for it is predictable that the general will won't predominate and that in the end domestic concerns absorb everything. Good laws lead to making better laws; bad laws bring about worse ones. Once someone says, "What do I care?" about the affairs of state, the state should be considered lost.

The cooling off of patriotism, the flurry of activity in the pursuit of private interest, the largeness of states, conquests, the abuse of government: these have suggested the route of using deputies or representatives of the people in the nation's assemblies. It is what in certain countries people dare call the third estate.[30] Thus the private interest of two orders is given first and second place; the public interest is given merely third place.

Sovereignty cannot be represented for the same reason that it cannot be alienated. It consists essentially in the general will, and the will does not allow of being represented. It is either itself or something else; there is nothing in between. The deputies of the people, therefore, neither are nor can be its representatives; they are merely its agents. They cannot conclude anything definitively. Any law that the people have not ratified in person is null; it is not a law at all. The English people believe themselves to be free. It is greatly mistaken; they are free only during the election of the members of parliament. Once these are elected, the people are enslaved; they are nothing. The use the English people make of that freedom in the brief moments of their liberty certainly warrants their losing it.

The idea of representatives is modern. It comes to us from feudal government, that iniquitous and absurd government in which the human race is degraded and the name of man is in dishonor. In the ancient republics and even in monarchies, the people never had representatives. The word itself was unknown. It is quite remarkable that in Rome where the tribunes were so sacred, no one even imagined that they could usurp the functions of the people, and that in the midst of such a great multitude, they never tried to pass a single plebiscite on their own authority. However, we can size up the difficulties that were sometimes caused by the crowd by what took place in the time of the Gracchi, when part of the citizenry voted from the rooftops.

Where right and liberty are everything, inconveniences are nothing. In the care of this wise people, everything was handled correctly. They allowed their lictors to do what their tribunes would not have dared to do. They had no fear that their lictors would want to represent them.

---

30. [Rousseau is thinking of France in particular. There in the Estates General (which did not meet between 1614 and the Revolution of 1789), the first estate was the clergy, the second the nobility, and the third the commoners. Because the estates voted separately, the clergy and nobility could outvote the commoners.]

However, to explain how the tribunes sometimes represented the people, it is enough to understand how the government represents the sovereign. Since the law is merely the declaration of the general will, it is clear that the people cannot be represented in the legislative power. But it can and should be represented in the executive power, which is merely force applied to the law. This demonstrates that, on close examination, very few nations would be found to have laws. Be that as it may, it is certain that, since they had no share in the executive power, the tribunes could never represent the Roman people by the rights of their office, but only by usurping those of the senate.

Among the Greeks, whatever the people had to do, they did by themselves. They were constantly assembled in the public square; they inhabited a mild climate; they were not greedy; their slaves did the work; their chief item of business was their liberty. No longer having the same advantages, how are the same rights to be preserved? Your harsher climates cause you to have more needs;[31] six months out of the year the public square is unsuitable for standing around; your muted tongues cannot make themselves understood in the open air; you pay more attention to your profits than to your liberty; and you are less fearful of slavery than you are of misery.

What! Can liberty be maintained only with the support of servitude? Perhaps. The two extremes meet. Everything that is not in nature has its drawbacks, and civil society more so than all the rest. There are some unfortunate circumstances where one's liberty can be preserved only at the expense of someone else's, and where the citizen can be perfectly free only if the slave is completely enslaved. Such was the situation in Sparta. As for you, modern peoples, you do not have slaves, but you yourselves are slaves. You pay for their liberty with your own. It is in vain that you crow about that preference. I find more cowardice in it than humanity.

I do not mean by all this that having slaves is necessary, nor that the right of slavery is legitimate, for I have proved the contrary. I am merely stating the reasons why modern peoples who believe themselves free have representatives, and why ancient peoples did not have them. Be that as it may, the moment a people gives itself representatives, they are no longer free; the people no longer exists.

All things considered, I do not see that it is possible henceforth for the sovereign to preserve among us the exercise of its rights, unless the city is

---

31. To adopt in cold countries the luxury and softness of the Orientals is to desire to be given their chains; it is submitting to these with even greater necessity than they did.

very small. But if it is very small, will it be subjugated? No. I will show later[32] how the external power of a great people can be combined with the ease of administration and the good order of a small state.

Chapter 16

That the Institution of Government Is Not a Contract

Once the legislative power has been well established, it is a matter of establishing the executive power in the same way. For this latter, which functions only by means of particular acts, not being of the essence of the former, is naturally separate from it. Were it possible for the sovereign, considered as such, to have the executive power, right and fact would be so completely confounded that we would no longer know what is law and what is not. And the body politic, thus denatured, would soon fall prey to the violence against which it was instituted.

Since the citizens are all equal by the social contract, what everyone should do can be prescribed by everyone. However, no one has the right to demand that someone else do what he does not do himself. Now it is precisely this right, indispensable for making the body politic live and move, that the sovereign gives the prince in instituting the government.

Several people have claimed that this act of establishment was a contract between the people and the leaders they gave themselves, a contract by which are stipulated between the two parties the conditions under which the one obliges itself to command and the other to obey.[33] It will be granted, I am sure, that this is a strange way of entering into a contract! But let us see if this opinion is tenable.

First, the supreme authority cannot be modified any more than it can be alienated; to limit it is to destroy it. It is absurd and contradictory for the sovereign to acquire a superior. To obligate oneself to obey a master is to return to full liberty.

---

32. This is what I intended to do in the rest of this work, when, in treating external relations, I would have come to confederations. An entirely new subject and its principles have yet to be established.

33. [This view was widespread in constitutionalist theory, and in the *Discourse on the Origin and Foundations of Inequality among Men*, Rousseau describes it as the generally held view. But it is not the view of Hobbes or Locke.]

Moreover, it is evident that this contract between the people and some or other persons would be a particular act. Whence it follows that this contract could be neither a law nor an act of sovereignty, and that consequently it would be illegitimate.

It is also clear that the contracting parties would, in relation to one another, be under only the law of nature and without any guarantee of their reciprocal commitments, which is contrary in every way to the civil state. Since the one who has force at his disposal is always in control of its employment, it would come to the same thing if we were to give the name contract to the act of a man who would say to another, "I am giving you all my goods on the condition that you give me back whatever you wish."

There is only one contract in the state, that of the association, and that alone excludes any other.[34] It is impossible to imagine any public contract that was not a violation of the first contract.

Chapter 17

On the Institution of the Government

What should be the terms under which we should conceive the act by which the government is instituted? I will begin by saying that this act is complex or composed of two others, namely, the establishment of the law and the execution of the law.

By the first, the sovereign decrees that there will be a governing body established under such and such a form. And it is clear that this act is a law.

By the second, the people name the leaders who will be placed in charge of the government that is being established. And since this nomination is a particular act, it is not a second law, but merely a consequence of the first and a function of the government.

The problem is to understand how there can be an act of government before a government exists, and how the people, who are only sovereign or subject, can in certain circumstances become prince or magistrate.

---

34. [Rousseau's target here is Samuel von Pufendorf's *Of the Law of Nature and Nations* (1672), which maintains that there is both a contract of association, which establishes the political community, and a contract of submission, which establishes the government.]

Moreover, it is here that we discover one of those remarkable properties of the body politic, by which it reconciles seemingly contradictory operations. For this takes place by a sudden conversion of sovereignty into democracy, so that, without any noticeable change, and solely by a new relation of all to all, the citizens, having become magistrates, pass from general to particular acts, and from the law to its execution.

This change of relation is not a speculative subtlety without exemplification in practice. It takes place every day in the English Parliament, where the lower chamber on certain occasions turns itself into a committee of the whole in order to discuss better the business of the sovereign court, thus becoming a simple commission, whereas the moment before it was the sovereign court, so that it later reports to itself, as the House of Commons, the result of what it has just settled in the committee of the whole, and deliberates all over again under one title about what it had already settled under another.

Thus the peculiar advantage of democratic government is that it can be established in actual fact by a simple act of the general will. After this, the provisional government remains in power, if this is the form adopted, or establishes in the name of the sovereign the government prescribed by the law; and thus everything is in accordance with the rule. It is not possible to institute the government in any other legitimate way without renouncing the principles established above.

Chapter 18

The Means of Preventing Usurpations of the Government

From these clarifications, it follows, in confirmation of Chapter 16, that the act that institutes the government is not a contract but a law; that the trustees of the executive power are not the masters of the people but their officers; that the people can establish and remove them when they please; that for the officers there is no question of contracting, but of obeying; and that in taking on the functions the state imposes on them, they merely fulfill their duty as citizens, without in any way having the right to dispute over the conditions.

Thus, when it happens that the people institute a hereditary government, whether it is monarchical within a single family or aristocratic within a class of citizens, this is not a commitment they are entering. It is a provisional form that they give the administration, until the people are pleased to order it otherwise.[35]

It is true that these changes are always dangerous, and that the established government should never be touched except when it becomes incompatible with the public good. But this circumspection is a maxim of politics and not a rule of law,[36] and the state is no more bound to leave civil authority to its leaders than it is to leave military authority to its generals.

Again, it is true that in such cases it is impossible to be too careful about observing all the formalities required in order to distinguish a regular and legitimate act from a seditious tumult, and the will of an entire people from the clamor of a faction. And it is here above all that one must not grant anything to odious cases[37] except what cannot be refused according to the full rigor of the law. And it is also from this obligation that the prince derives a great advantage in preserving his power in spite of the people, without anyone being able to say that he has usurped it. For in appearing to use only his rights, it is quite easy for him to extend them, and, under the pretext of public peace, to prevent assemblies destined to reestablish good order. Thus he avails himself of a silence he keeps from being broken, or of irregularities he causes to be committed, to assume that the opinion of those who are silenced by fear is supportive of him, and to punish those who dare to speak. This is how the decemvirs, having been first elected for one year and then continued for another year, tried to retain their power in perpetuity by no longer permitting the comitia to assemble. And it is by this simple means that all the governments of the world, once armed with the public force, sooner or later usurp the public authority.

---

35. [The word "provisional" was seized on by the Genevan authorities when they condemned the *Social Contract* as being destructive of all stability in government.]
36. [Rousseau's word is *droit* (often, as here in the subtitle to the *Social Contract*, "right"). In French, *droit* and *loi* (law) have meanings that overlap much more extensively than law and right in English, so that "law" is often the only possible translation of *droit*. Thus in France one takes a degree *en droit* (in law) and studies in the *faculté de droit* (faculty of law). The French for "the law of nature" is *le droit naturel*, for "the law of nations" it is *le droit des gens*, and for "the law of war" it is *le droit de guerre*.]
37. ["Odious cases" refers to the principle of Roman law *odia restringenda, favores ampliandi*: when someone claims a right that will have beneficial consequences, the law should be interpreted liberally; but when they claim a right that will have evil ("odious") consequences, the law should be interpreted as narrowly as possible.]

The periodic assemblies I have spoken of earlier are suited to the prevention or postponement of this misfortune, especially when they have no need for a formal convocation. For then the prince could not prevent them without openly declaring himself a violator of the laws and an enemy of the state. The opening of these assemblies, which have as their sole object the preservation of the social treaty, should always take place through two propositions that can never be suppressed, and that are voted on separately:

The first: *Does it please the sovereign to preserve the present form of government?*

The second: *Does it please the people to leave their administration to those who are now in charge of it?*[38]

I am presupposing here what I believe I have demonstrated, namely that in the state there is no fundamental law that cannot be revoked, not even the social compact. For if all the citizens were to assemble in order to break this compact by common agreement, no one could doubt that it was legitimately broken. Grotius[39] even thinks that each person can renounce the state of which he is a member and recover his natural liberty and his goods by leaving the country.[40] But it would be absurd that all the citizens together could not do what each of them can do separately.

END OF THE THIRD BOOK

---

38. [The Genevan authorities took particular offense at this. It looked to them like an invitation to periodic revolutions.]

39. [Grotius, *Law of War and Peace*, bk. 2, ch. 5, §24. Grotius himself limits this right as Rousseau does in his note.]

40. On the understanding that one does not leave in order to evade one's duty and to be exempt from serving the homeland at a time when it has need of us. In such circumstances, taking flight would be criminal and punishable; it would no longer be withdrawal, but desertion.

BOOK IV

Chapter 1

That the General Will Is Indestructible

As long as several men together consider themselves to be a single body, they have but a single will, which is concerned with their common preservation and the general well-being. Then all the energies of the state are vigorous and simple; its maxims are clear and luminous; there are no entangled, contradictory interests; the common good is clearly apparent everywhere, demanding only good sense in order to be perceived. Peace, union, equality are enemies of political subtleties. Upright and simple men are difficult to deceive on account of their simplicity. Traps and clever pretexts do not fool them. They are not even clever enough to be duped. When, among the happiest people in the world, bands of peasants are seen regulating their affairs of state under an oak tree[1] and always acting wisely, can one help scorning the refinements of other nations, which make themselves illustrious and miserable with so much art and mystery?

A state thus governed needs very few laws; and in proportion as it becomes necessary to promulgate new ones, this necessity is universally understood. The first to propose them merely says what everybody has already felt; and there is no question of either intrigues or eloquence to secure the passage into law of what each has already resolved to do, once he is sure the others will do likewise.

What misleads argumentative types is the fact that, since they take into account only states that were badly constituted from the beginning, they are struck by the impossibility of maintaining such an administration in them. They laugh when they imagine all the foolishness a clever knave or a sly orator could get the people of Paris or London to believe. They do not know that Cromwell would have been sentenced to hard

---

1. [A reference to the rural cantons of Switzerland.]

labor by the people of Berne, and the Duke of Beaufort imprisoned by the Genevans.[2]

But when the social bond begins to relax and the state to grow weak, when private interests begin to make themselves felt and small societies begin to influence the large one, the common interest changes and finds opponents. Unanimity no longer reigns in the votes; the general will is no longer the will of all. Contradictions and debates arise, and the best advice does not pass without disputes.

Finally, when the state, on the verge of ruin, subsists only in an illusory and vain form, when the social bond of unity is broken in all hearts, when the meanest interest brazenly appropriates the sacred name of the public good, then the general will becomes mute. Everyone, guided by secret motives, no more expresses his opinion as a citizen than if the state had never existed; and iniquitous decrees having as their sole purpose the private interest are falsely passed under the name of laws.

Does it follow from this that the general will is annihilated or corrupted? No, it is always constant, unalterable, and pure; but it is subordinate to other wills that prevail over it. Each man, in detaching his interest from the common interest, clearly sees that he cannot totally separate himself from it; but his share of the public misfortune seems insignificant to him compared to the exclusive good he intends to make his own. Apart from this private good, he wants the general good in his own interest, just as strongly as anyone else. Even in selling his vote for money he does not extinguish the general will in himself; he evades it. The error he commits is that of changing the thrust of the question and answering a different question from the one he was asked. Thus, instead of saying through his vote, "It is advantageous to the state," he says, "It is advantageous to this man or that party that this or that view should pass." Thus the law of the public order in the assemblies is not so much to maintain the general will there, as to bring it about that it is always questioned and that it always answers.

I could present here a number of reflections on the simple right to vote in every act of sovereignty, a right that nothing can take away from the citizens, and on the right to state an opinion, to offer proposals, to divide, to discuss, which the government always takes great care to allow only to its

---

2. [The Duke of Beaufort (1594–1665) was an illegitimate son of Henry IV; he was twice accused of conspiring to assassinate Richelieu and was exiled, first to Holland and then to England.]

members.[3] But this important subject would require a separate treatise, and I cannot say everything in this one.

Chapter 2

On Voting

It is clear from the preceding chapter that the manner in which general business is taken care of can provide a rather accurate indication of the present state of mores and of the health of the body politic. The more harmony reigns in the assemblies, that is to say, the closer opinions come to unanimity, the more dominant too is the general will. But long debates, dissensions, and tumult betoken the ascendance of private interests and the decline of the state.

This seems less evident when two or more orders enter into its constitution, such as the patricians and the plebeians in Rome, whose quarrels often disturbed the comitia, even in the best of times in the republic. But this exception is more apparent than real. For then, by the vice inherent in the body politic, there are, as it were, two states in one. What is not true of the two together is true of each of them separately. And indeed even in the most tumultuous times, the plebiscites of the people, when the senate did not interfere with them, always passed quietly and by a large majority of votes. Since the citizens have but one interest, the people had but one will.

At the other extreme of the circle, unanimity returns. It is when the citizens, having fallen into servitude, no longer have either liberty or will. Then fear and flattery turn voting into acclamation. People no longer deliberate; either they adore or they curse. Such was the vile manner in which

---

3. [Here Rousseau seemingly limits the sovereign's right to the right to vote, giving the government a monopoly of proposing legislation and speaking in the assembly. This corresponds to the Genevan constitution, in which the little council controlled the agenda of the general council, and he approves this arrangement in his dedication to the *Discourse on the Origin of Inequality*. It also corresponds to the Venetian constitution in which the Grand Council voted but did not debate. But this is not the view he takes elsewhere in *On the Social Contract* or in the *Letters Written from the Mountain* (1764).]

the senate expressed its opinions under the emperors; sometimes it did so with ridiculous precautions. Tacitus observes that under Otho, the senators, while heaping curses upon Vitellius, contrived at the same time to make a frightful noise, so that, if by chance he became master, he would be unable to know what each of them had said.[4]

From these various considerations there arise the maxims by which the manner of counting votes and comparing opinions should be regulated, depending on whether the general will is more or less easy to know and the state more or less in decline.

There is but one law that by its nature requires unanimous consent. This is the social compact. For civil association is the most voluntary act in the world. Since every man is born free and master of himself, no one can, under any pretext whatever, place another under subjection without his consent.[5] To decide that the son of a slave is born a slave is to decide that he is not born a man.[6]

If, therefore, at the time of the social compact, there are opponents to it, their opposition does not invalidate the contract; it merely prevents them from being included in it. They are foreigners among citizens. Once the state is instituted, residency implies consent. To inhabit the territory is to submit to sovereignty.[7]

Aside from this primitive contract, the vote of the majority always obligates all the others. This is a consequence of the contract itself. But it is asked how a man can be both free and forced to conform to wills that are not his own. How can the opponents be both free and placed in subjection to laws to which they have not consented?

I answer that the question is not put properly. The citizen consents to all the laws, even to those that pass in spite of his opposition, and even to those that punish him when he dares to violate any of them. The constant will of all the members of the state is the general will; through it they are citizens

4. [Tacitus, *Histories*, bk. 1, ch. 85.]
5. [Cf. Locke, *Two Treatises*, Second Treatise, §§95, 99.]
6. [This may be thought to follow from Locke's argument, but Locke never explicitly states this conclusion, and Rousseau is unique among major eighteenth-century political theorists in his systematic opposition to slavery.]
7. This should always be understood in connection with a free state, for otherwise his family, his goods, the impossibility of claiming asylum, necessity, or violence can keep an inhabitant in a country in spite of himself; and then his sojourn alone no longer presupposes his consent to the contract or to the violation of the contract.

and free.[8] When a law is proposed in the people's assembly, what is asked of them is not, to be precise, whether they approve or reject the proposition, but whether or not it conforms to the general will that is theirs. Each man, in giving his vote, states his opinion on this matter, and the declaration of the general will is drawn from the counting of votes. When, therefore, the opinion contrary to mine prevails, this proves merely that I was in error, and that what I took to be the general will was not so. If my private opinion had prevailed, I would have done something other than what I had wanted. In that case I would not have been free.

This presupposes, it is true, that all the characteristics of the general will are still in the majority. When they cease to be there, there is no longer any liberty regardless of the side one takes.

In showing earlier how private wills were substituted for the general will in public deliberations, I have given an adequate indication of the possible ways of preventing this abuse. I will discuss this again at a later time. With respect to the proportional number of votes needed to declare this will, I have also given the principles on the basis of which it can be determined. The difference of a single vote breaks a tie vote; a single opponent destroys a unanimous vote. But between a unanimous and a tie vote there are several unequal divisions, at any of which this proportionate number can be fixed in accordance with the condition and needs of the body politic.

Two general maxims can serve to regulate these ratios: one, that the more important and serious the deliberations are, the closer the prevailing opinion should be to unanimity; the other, that the more the matter at hand calls for speed, the smaller the prescribed difference in the division of opinion should be. In decisions that must be reached immediately, a majority of a single vote should suffice. The first of these maxims seems more suited to the laws, and the second to public business. Be that as it may, it is the combination of the two that establishes the ratios that best help the majority to render its decision.

---

8. In Genoa, the word *libertas* [liberty] can be read on the front of prisons and on the chains of galley slaves. This application of the motto is fine and just. Indeed it is only malefactors of all social classes who prevent the citizen from being free. In a country where all such people were in the galleys, the most perfect liberty would be enjoyed.

Chapter 3

On Elections

With regard to the elections of the prince and the magistrates, which are, as I have said, complex acts, there are two ways to proceed, namely, by choice or by lots. Both of these have been used in various republics, and at present we still see a very complicated mixture of the two in the election of the Doge of Venice.

"Voting by lot," says Montesquieu, "is of the essence of democracy." I agree, but why is this the case? "Drawing lots," he continues, "is a way of electing that harms no one; it leaves each citizen a reasonable hope of serving the homeland."[9] These are not reasons.

If we keep in mind that the election of leaders is a function of government and not of sovereignty, we will see why the method of drawing lots is more in the nature of democracy, where the administration is all the better the fewer decisions it makes.

In every true democracy the magistracy is not an advantage but a heavy burden that cannot justly be imposed on one private individual rather than another. The law alone can impose this burden on the one to whom it falls by lot. For in that case, with the condition being equal for all and the choice not depending on any human will, there is no particular application that alters the universality of the law.

In any aristocracy, the prince chooses the prince; the government is preserved by itself, and it is there that voting is appropriate.

The example of the election of the Doge of Venice, far from destroying this distinction, confirms it. This mixed procedure suits a mixed government. For it is an error to regard the government of Venice as a true aristocracy. For although the people there have no part in the government, the nobility is itself the people. A multitude of poor Barnabites[10] never come[11] near any magistracy and have nothing to show for their nobility but the vain title of excellency and the right to be present at the grand council. Since

---

9. [Montesquieu, *Spirit of the Laws*, bk. 2, ch. 2.]
10. [This was the name for the poor nobles of Venice, generally said to refer to the area around the Church of St. Barnabas, where they lived, but also presumably a reference to St. Barnabas himself, who sold all he had and gave it to the apostles.]
11. [The text of the first edition is *approcha* (past tense), but as the rest of the passage is in the present tense this seems likely to be a misprint for *approche* (present tense).]

this grand council is as numerous as our general council in Geneva,[12] its illustrious members have no more privileges than our simple citizens. It is certain that, aside from the extreme disparity between the two republics, the bourgeoisie of Geneva exactly corresponds to the Venetian patriciate. Our natives and inhabitants correspond to the citizens[13] and people of Venice. Our peasants correspond to the subjects on the mainland. Finally, whatever way one considers this republic, apart from its size, its government is no more aristocratic than ours. The whole difference lies in the fact that, since we do not have leaders who serve for life, we do not have the same need to draw lots.

Elections by lot would have few disadvantages in a true democracy, where, all things being equal both in mores and talents as well as in maxims and fortunes, the choice would become almost indifferent. But I have already said there is no such thing as a true democracy.

When choice and lots are mixed, the former should fill the positions requiring special talents, such as military posts. The latter is suited to those positions, such as judicial offices, where good sense, justice, and integrity are enough, because in a well-constituted state these qualities are common to all the citizens.

Neither the drawing of lots nor voting has any place in a monarchical government. Since the monarch is by right the only prince and sole magistrate, the choice of his lieutenants belongs to him alone. When the Abbot of Saint-Pierre proposed multiplying the Councils of the King of France and electing the members by ballot, he did not realize that he was proposing to change the form of government.[14]

It remains for me to speak of the manner in which the votes are cast and counted in the people's assembly. But perhaps in this regard the chronicle of the Roman system of administration will explain more clearly all the maxims I could establish. It is not beneath the dignity of a judicious reader to consider in some detail how public and private business was conducted in a council made of two hundred thousand men.

---

12. [The Grand Council had, according to Rousseau in his *Considerations on the Government of Poland*, 1,200 members.]
13. [The citizens or *cittadini* of Venice, whose status was below that of the nobility (who alone exercised political rights). The citizens had a monopoly of administrative positions.]
14. [Rousseau, at the instigation of his employer Mme Dupin, wrote at length on the political theory of the abbot of Saint-Pierre.]

Chapter 4

On the Roman Comitia[15]

We have no especially reliable records of the earliest period of Rome's history. It even appears quite likely that most of the things reported about it are fables.[16] And in general the most instructive part of the annals of peoples, which is the history of their founding, is the part we most lack. Experience teaches us every day the causes that lead to the revolutions of empires. But since peoples are no longer being formed, we have almost nothing but conjecture to explain how they were formed.

The customs we find established attest at the very least to the fact that these customs had an origin. Of the traditions that go back to these origins, those that are supported by the greatest authorities and that are confirmed by the strongest reasons should pass for the most certain. These are the maxims I have tried to follow in attempting to find out how the freest and most powerful people on earth exercised their supreme power.

After the founding of Rome, the newborn republic, that is, the army of the founder, composed of Albans, Sabines, and foreigners, was divided into three classes, which took the name *tribus* [thirds or tribes] from this division. Each of these tribes was divided into ten curiae, and each curia into *decuriae*, at the head of which were placed leaders called *curiones* and *decuriones*.

Moreover, from each tribe was drawn a body of one hundred horsemen or knights, called a *century*. It is clear from this that these divisions, being hardly necessary in a market town, originally were exclusively military. But it appears that an instinct for greatness led the small town of Rome to provide itself in advance with a system of administration suited to the capital of the world.

One disadvantage soon resulted from this initial division. With the tribes of the Albans[17] and the Sabines[18] always remaining constant, while that of

---

15. [Rousseau's main source in this chapter is Carlo Sigonio, *De antiquo jure civium Romanorum* (1560).]

16. The name *Rome*, which people say comes from *Romulus*, is Greek, and means *force*. The name *Numa* is also Greek, and means *law*. What is the likelihood that the first two kings of that town would have borne in advance names so clearly related to what they did?

17. Ramnenses.

18. Tatienses.

the foreigners[19] grew continually, thanks to their perpetual influx, this latter group soon outnumbered the other two. The remedy that Servius found for this dangerous abuse was to change the division and, in place of the division based on blood, which he abolished, to substitute another division drawn from the areas of the town occupied by each tribe. In place of the three tribes, he made four. Each of them occupied one of the hills of Rome and bore its name. Thus, in remedying the inequality of the moment, he also prevented it from happening in the future. And in order that this division might not be merely one of localities but of men, he prohibited the inhabitants of one quarter from moving into another, which prevented the bloodlines from mingling with one another.

He also doubled the three ancient centuries of horsemen and added to them twelve others, but always under the old names, a simple and judicious means by which he achieved the differentiation of the body of knights from that of the people, without causing the latter to murmur.

To the four urban tribes, Servius added fifteen others called rural tribes, because they were formed from the inhabitants of the countryside, divided into the same number of cantons. Subsequently, the same number of new ones were brought into being, and the Roman people finally found itself divided into thirty-five tribes, a number at which they remained fixed until the end of the republic.

There resulted from this distinction between the tribes of the city and those of the countryside an effect worth noting, because there is no other example of it, and because Rome owed to it both the preservation of its mores and the growth of its empire. One might have thought that the urban tribes soon would have arrogated to themselves power and honors, and would have wasted no time in vilifying the rural tribes. What took place was quite the opposite. The early Romans' taste for country life is well known. They inherited this taste from the wise founder who united liberty with rural and military labors and, so to speak, relegated to the town arts, crafts, intrigue, fortune, and slavery.

Thus, since all the illustrious men in Rome lived in the country and tilled the soil, people became accustomed to look only there for the mainstays of the republic. Since this condition was that of the worthiest patricians, it was honored by everyone. The simple and laborious life of the villagers was preferred to the lazy and idle life of the bourgeois of Rome. And someone who would have been merely a miserable proletarian in the town became a respected citizen as a field worker. It was not without reason, said Varro, that

---

19. Luceres.

our great-souled ancestors established in the village the nursery of those robust and valiant men who defended them in time of war and nourished them in time of peace. Pliny says positively that the tribes of the fields were honored on account of the men who made them up; however, cowards whom men wished to vilify were transferred in disgrace to the tribes of the town. When the Sabine Appius Claudius came to settle in Rome, he was decked with honors and inscribed in a rural tribe that later took the name of his family. Finally, freedmen all entered the urban tribes, never the rural ones. And during the entire period of the republic, there was not a single example of any of these freedmen reaching any magistracy, even if he had become a citizen.

This maxim was excellent, but it was pushed so far that it finally resulted in a change and certainly an abuse in the administration.

First, the censors, after having long arrogated to themselves the right to transfer citizens arbitrarily from one tribe to another, permitted most of them to have themselves inscribed in whatever tribe they pleased. Certainly this permission served no useful purpose and deprived the censorship of one of its greatest resources. Moreover, with the great and the powerful having themselves inscribed in the tribes of the countryside, and the freedmen who had become citizens remaining with the populace in the tribes of the town, the tribes in general no longer had either place or territory. On the contrary, they all found themselves so intermixed that the members of each could no longer be identified except by the registers, so that in this way the idea of the word *tribe* shifted from referring to location to referring to persons, or rather it became almost a chimera.

In addition, it happened that since the tribes of the town were nearer at hand, they were often the strongest in the comitia, and sold the state to those who deigned to buy the votes of the mob that composed them.

Regarding the curiae, since the founder had created ten curiae in each tribe, the entire Roman people, who were then contained within the town walls, were composed of thirty curiae, each of which had its temples, its gods, its officials, its priests, and its feasts called *compitalia*, similar to the *paganalia* later held by the rural tribes.

When Servius established this new division, since this number thirty could not be divided equally among his four tribes, and since he did not want to alter it, the curiae became another division of the inhabitants of Rome, independent of the tribes. But there was no question of the curiae either in the rural tribes or among the people that composed them; for since the tribes had become a purely civil establishment and another system of administration had been introduced for the raising of troops, the military divisions of Romulus were found to be superfluous. Thus, even though every citizen was inscribed in a tribe, there were plenty who were not inscribed in a curia.

Servius established still a third division, which bore no relationship to the two preceding ones and which became, in its effects, the most important of all. He divided the entire Roman people into six classes, which he distinguished neither by place nor by person, but by wealth. Thus the first classes were filled by the rich, the last by the poor, and the middle ones by those who enjoyed a moderate fortune. These six classes were subdivided into 193 other bodies called centuries, and these bodies were distributed in such a manner that the first class alone contained more than half of them, and the last contained only one. Thus it was that the class with the smallest number of men was the one with the greatest number of centuries and that the entire last class counted only as a single subdivision, even though it alone contained more than half the inhabitants of Rome.

In order that the people might have less of a grasp of the consequences of this last form, Servius feigned giving it a military air. He placed in the second class two centuries of armorers, and two centuries of artillery in the fourth. In each class, with the exception of the last, he made a distinction between the young and the old, that is to say, between those who were obliged to carry arms and those whose age exempted them by law. This distinction, more than that of wealth, produced the necessity for frequently retaking the census or roll call. Finally, he wished that the assembly would be held in the Campus Martius, and that all those who were of age to serve should come there with their arms.

The reason he did not follow this same division of young and old in the last class is that the populace of which it was composed were not accorded the honor of bearing arms for the homeland. It was necessary to possess a hearth in order to obtain the right to defend it. And of the innumerable troops of beggars who today grace the armies of kings, there is perhaps no one who would not have been disdainfully chased from a Roman cohort, when the soldiers were the defenders of liberty.

In addition there was a distinction in the last class between the *proletarians* and those that are called *capite censi*. The former, not completely reduced to nothing, at least gave citizens to the state, sometimes even soldiers in times of pressing need. As for those who possessed nothing at all and could be reckoned only by counting heads, they were regarded as absolutely worthless, and Marius was the first who deigned to enroll them.

Without deciding here whether this third method of reckoning was good or bad in itself, I believe I can affirm that it could be made practicable only by the simple mores of the early Romans, their disinterestedness, their taste for agriculture, their dislike for commerce and for the passion for profits. Where is the modern people among whom their devouring greed, their unsettled spirit, their intrigue, their continual displacements, their perpetual revolutions of fortunes could allow such an establishment to last twenty years without overturning the entire state? It must also be duly noted that the mores and the censorship, which were stronger than this institution, corrected its defects in Rome, and that a rich man found himself relegated to the class of the poor for having made too much of a show of his wealth.

From all this, it is easy to grasp why mention is almost never made of more than five classes, even though there were actually six. The sixth, since it furnished neither soldiers for the army nor voters for the Campus Martius[20] and was virtually of no use in the republic, was hardly ever counted for anything.

Such were the various divisions of the Roman people. Let us now look at the effect these divisions had on the assemblies. When legitimately convened, these assemblies were called *comitia*. Ordinarily they were held in the Roman forum or in the Campus Martius, and were distinguished as *comitia curiata, comitia centuriata*, and *comitia tributa*, according to which of the three forms was the basis on which they were organized. The *comitia curiata* were based on the institution of Romulus, the *comitia centuriata* on that of Servius, and the *comitia tributa* on that of the tribunes of the people. No law received sanction, no magistrate was elected save in the comitia. And since there was no citizen who was not inscribed in a curia, a century, or a tribe, it followed that no citizen was excluded from the right of suffrage and that the Roman people were truly sovereign both de jure and de facto.

For the comitia to be legitimately assembled and for what took place to have the force of law, three conditions had to be met: first, the body or the magistrate who called these assemblies had to be invested with the necessary authority to do so; second, the assembly had to be held on one of the days permitted by law; third, the auguries had to be favorable.

The reason for the first regulation needs no explanation. The second is an administrative matter. Thus the comitia were not allowed to be held on holidays and on market days, when people from the country, coming to Rome on business, did not have time to spend the day in the public forum. By means of the third rule, the senate held in check a proud and restless

---

20. I say *Campus Martius* because it was here that the *comitia centuriata* gathered. In the two other forms of assembly, the people gathered in the *forum* or elsewhere, and then the *capite censi* had as much influence and authority as the first citizens.

people and appropriately tempered the ardor of seditious tribunes. But these latter found more than one way of getting around this constraint.

The laws and the election of leaders were not the only matters submitted to the judgment of the comitia. Since the Roman people had usurped the most important functions of the government,[21] it can be said that the fate of Europe was decided in its assemblies. This variety of objects gave rise to the various forms these assemblies took on according to the matters on which they had to pronounce.

In order to judge these various forms, it is enough to compare them. In instituting the curiae, Romulus had intended to contain the senate by means of the people and the people by means of the senate, while he dominated both equally. He therefore gave the people, by means of this form, all the authority of number to balance that of power and wealth that he left to the patricians. But in conformity with the spirit of the monarchy, he nevertheless left a greater advantage to the patricians through their clients' influence on the majority of the votes. This admirable institution of patrons and clients was a masterpiece of politics and humanity, without which the patriciate, so contrary to the spirit of the republic, could not have subsisted. Only Rome had the honor of giving the world this fine example, which never led to any abuse, and which, for all that, has never been copied.

Since this same form of curiae had subsisted under the kings until Servius, and since the reign of the last Tarquin was not considered legitimate, royal laws were generally known by the name *leges curiatae*.

Under the republic, the curiae, always limited to the four urban tribes and including no more than the populace of Rome, were unable to suit either the senate, which was at the head of the patricians, or the tribunes, who, plebeians though they were, were at the head of the citizens who were in comfortable circumstances. The curiae therefore fell into discredit and their degradation was such that their thirty assembled lictors together did what the *comitia curiata* should have done.

The division by centuries was so favorable to the aristocracy that at first it is difficult to see how the senate did not always prevail in the comitia that bears this name and by which the consuls, the censors, and other curule

---

21. [Since, according to Rousseau's political theory, the sovereign people always have the right to reclaim power from the government, the word "usurped" should be read as if in scare quotation marks. The word is evidently not used carelessly, however, as Rousseau repeats it in a reference to this passage in *Letters Written from the Mountain* (1764). Evidently he thought it a mistake for the people to exercise too many of the functions of government.]

magistrates were elected. In fact, of the 193 centuries that formed the six classes of the entire Roman people, the first class contained 98, and, since the voting was counted by centuries only, this first class alone prevailed in the number of votes over all the rest. When all its centuries were in agreement, they did not even continue to count the votes. Decisions made by the smallest number passed for a decision of the multitude; and it can be said that in the *comitia centuriata* business was settled more by who had the most money than by who had the most votes.

But this extreme authority was tempered in two ways. First, since ordinarily the tribunes, and always a large number of plebeians, were in the class of the rich, they balanced the authority of the patricians in this first class.

The second way consisted in the following. Instead of at the outset making the centuries vote according to their order, which would have meant always beginning with the first, one century was chosen by lot, and that one[22] alone proceeded to the election. After this, all the centuries were called on another day according to their rank, repeated the same election, and usually confirmed it. Thus the authority of example was removed from rank in order to give it to lot, in accordance with the principle of democracy.

There resulted from this custom still another advantage, namely that the citizens from the country had time between the two elections to inform themselves of the merit of the provisionally named candidate, so that they did not have to vote without knowledge of what was at stake.

But on the pretext of speeding things up, this custom was finally abolished and the two elections were held on the same day.

Strictly speaking, the *comitia tributa* were the council of the Roman people. They were convened only by the tribunes. The tribunes were elected and passed their plebiscites there. Not only did the senate hold no rank in them, it did not even have the right to be present. And since the senators were forced to obey the laws upon which they could not vote, they were less free in this regard than the humblest citizens. This injustice was altogether ill conceived, and was by itself enough to invalidate the decrees of a body to which none of its members were admitted. If all the patricians had been present at these comitia by virtue of the right they had as citizens, having then become simple private individuals, they would not have had a great deal of influence on a form of voting that was tallied by counting heads and

---

22. This century, having been chosen thus by lot, was called *prae rogativa*, on account of the fact that it was the first to be asked for its vote, and it is from this that the word *prerogative* is derived.

where the humblest proletarian had as much clout as the leading figure in the senate.

Thus it can be seen that besides the order that resulted from these various distributions for gathering the votes of so great a people, these distributions were not reducible to forms indifferent in themselves, but each one had effects relative to the viewpoints that caused it to be preferred.

Without going further into greater detail here, it is a consequence of the preceding clarifications that the *comitia tributa* were the most favorable to the popular government, and the *comitia centuriata* most favorable to the aristocracy. Regarding the *comitia curiata*, in which the populace of Rome alone formed the majority, since these were good only for favoring tyranny and evil designs, they fell of their own weight into disrepute, and even the seditious abstained from using a means that made their real intent only too apparent. It is certain that all the majesty of the Roman people is found only in the *comitia centuriata*, which alone were complete, given that the *comitia curiata* lacked the rural tribes, and the *comitia tributa* lacked the senate and the patricians.

As for the manner of collecting the votes, among the early Romans it was as simple as their mores, though not as simple as in Sparta. Each gave his vote in a loud voice, and a clerk marked it down accordingly. The majority vote in each tribe determined the tribe's vote; the majority vote of the tribes determined the people's vote; and the same went for the curiae and the centuries. This custom was good as long as honesty reigned among the citizens and each was ashamed to cast his vote publicly in favor of an unjust proposal or an unworthy subject. But when the people became corrupt and votes were bought, it was fitting that they should cast their votes in secret in order to restrain the buyers through distrust and to provide scoundrels the means of not being traitors.

I know that Cicero condemns this change and attributes the ruin of the republic partly to it.[23] But although I am aware of the weight that Cicero's authority should have here, I cannot agree with him. On the contrary, I think that, by not having made enough changes of this sort, the fall of the state was accelerated. Just as the regimen of healthy people is not suitable for the sick, one should not want to govern a corrupt people by means of the same laws that are suited to a good people. Nothing proves this maxim better than the long life of the Republic of Venice, whose shadow still exists, solely because its laws are suited only to wicked men.

---

23. [Cf. Montesquieu, *Spirit of the Laws*, bk. 2, ch. 2.]

Tablets were therefore distributed to the citizens by means of which each man could vote without anyone knowing what his opinion was. New formalities were also established for collecting the tablets, counting the votes, comparing the numbers, and so on. None of this prevented the integrity of the officials in charge of these functions[24] from often being under suspicion. Finally, to prevent intrigue and vote trafficking, edicts were passed whose sheer multiplicity is proof of their uselessness.

Toward the end of the period of the republic, it was often necessary to have recourse to extraordinary expedients in order to make up for the inadequacy of the laws. Sometimes miracles were alleged. But this means, which could deceive the people, did not deceive those who governed them. Sometimes an assembly was unexpectedly convened before the candidates had time to carry out their intrigues. Sometimes an entire session was spent on talk, when it was clear that the people were won over and ready to take the wrong side on an issue. But finally ambition eluded everything; and what is unbelievable is that in the midst of so much abuse, this immense people, by virtue of its ancient regulations, did not cease to choose magistrates, pass laws, judge cases, or expedite private and public business, almost as easily as the senate itself could have done.

Chapter 5

On the Tribunate

When it is not possible to establish an exact proportion between the constitutive parts of the state, or when indestructible causes continually alter the relationships between them, a special magistracy is then established that does not make up yet another body alongside them. This magistracy restores each term to its true relationship to the others, and creates a link or a middle term either between the prince and the people or between the prince and the sovereign, or on both sides at once, if necessary.

This body, which I will call the *tribunate*, is the preserver of the laws and the legislative power. It serves sometimes to protect the sovereign against the government, as the tribunes of the people did in Rome; sometimes to sustain the government against the people, as the Council of Ten now does

---

24. Custodes, diribitores, rogatores suffragiorum.

in Venice; and sometimes to maintain equilibrium between the two, as the ephors did in Sparta.

The tribunate is not a constitutive part of the city and it should have no share in either the legislative or the executive power. But this is precisely what makes its own power the greater. For although it is unable to do anything, it can prevent everything. It is more sacred and more revered as a defender of the laws than the prince who executes them and the sovereign who gives them. This was very clearly apparent in Rome when the proud patricians, who always scorned the entire people, were forced to bow before a humble official of the people, who had neither auspices nor jurisdiction.

A well-tempered tribunate is the firmest support of a good constitution. But if it has the slightest bit too much force, it undermines everything. As for weakness, there is none in its nature; and provided it is something, it is never less than it ought to be.

It degenerates into tyranny when it usurps the executive power, of which it is merely the moderator, and when it wants to dispense from the laws it ought only to protect.[25] The enormous power of the ephors, which was without danger as long as Sparta preserved its mores, hastened corruption once it had begun. The blood of Agis, who was slaughtered by these tyrants, was avenged by his successor. The crime and the punishment of the ephors equally hastened the fall of the republic; and after Cleomenes, Sparta was no longer anything. Rome also perished in the same way, and the excessive power of the tribunes, which they had gradually usurped, finally served, with the help of the laws that were made to protect liberty, as a safeguard for the emperors who destroyed it. As for the Council of Ten in Venice, it is a bloody tribunal, equally horrifying to the patricians and the people, and which, far from proudly protecting the laws, no longer serves any purpose, after their degradation, beyond that of delivering blows in the dark that no one dares notice.[26]

Just like the government, the tribunate is weakened as a result of the multiplication of its members. When the tribunes of the Roman people, who at first were two in number, then five, wanted to double this number,

---

25. [Rousseau's phrase is *dispenser les loix*. Vaughan and the Pléiade edition interpret this as meaning *administrer les loix* (administer the laws), but I cannot find an equivalent usage in contemporary (or indeed any) dictionaries or elsewhere in Rousseau, and it seems likely that it is a misprint for *dispenser des loix* (dispense from the laws)—a reading adopted by the Hachette edition.]

26. [This account of contemporary Venice as a species of tyranny follows on a long line of previous commentators, including Montesquieu.]

the senate let them do so, certain that one faction could be used to hold the other in check; and this did not fail to happen.

The best way to prevent usurpations by so formidable a body, one that no government has yet made use of, would be not to make this body permanent, but to regulate the intervals during which it would be suppressed. These intervals, which ought not be so long as to allow abuses time to grow in strength, can be fixed by law in such a way that it is easy to shorten them, as needed, by means of extraordinary commissions.

This way seems to me to have no disadvantage, for since, as I have said, the tribunate is not part of the constitution, it can be set aside without doing the constitution any harm; and it seems bound to be effective because a newly reestablished magistrate begins not with the power his predecessor had, but with the power the law gives him.

Chapter 6

On Dictatorship[27]

The inflexibility of the laws, which prevents them from adapting to circumstances, can in certain instances make them harmful and render them the instrument of the state's downfall in time of crisis. The order and the slowness of formal procedures require a space of time that circumstances sometimes do not permit. A thousand eventualities can present themselves, which the legislator has not foreseen, and it is a very necessary bit of foresight to realize that not everything can be foreseen.

It is therefore necessary to avoid the desire to strengthen political institutions to the point of removing the power to suspend their effect. Sparta itself allowed its laws to lie dormant.

But only the greatest dangers can counterbalance the danger of altering the public order, and the sacred power of the laws should never be suspended except when it is a question of the safety of the homeland. In these rare and obvious cases, public safety can be provided for by a special act that confers the responsibility for it on someone who is most worthy. This commission can be carried out in two ways, according to the type of danger.

---

27. [This chapter is clearly under the influence of Machiavelli, *Discourses*, bk. 1, chs. 34–35.]

If increasing the activity of government is enough to remedy the situation, it is concentrated in one or two of its members. Thus it is not the authority of the laws that is altered, but merely the form of their administration. But if the peril is such that the apparatus of the laws is an obstacle to their being protected from it, then a supreme leader is named who silences all the laws and briefly suspends the sovereign authority. In such a case, the general will is not in doubt, and it is evident that the first intention of the people is that the state should not perish. In this manner, the suspension of legislative authority does not abolish it. The magistrate who silences it cannot make it speak; he dominates it without being able to represent it. He can do anything but make laws.

The first way was used by the Roman senate when, by a sacred formula, it entrusted the consuls with the responsibility for providing for the safety of the republic. The second took place when one of the two consuls named a dictator,[28] a custom for which Alba had provided Rome the precedent.

In the beginning days of the republic, there was frequent recourse to dictatorship, since the state did not yet have a sufficiently stable basis to be capable of sustaining itself by the force of its constitution. Since the mores at that time made many of the precautions superfluous that would have been necessary in other times, there was no fear either that a dictator would abuse his authority or that he would try to hold on to it beyond his term of office. On the contrary, it seemed that such a great power was a burden to the one in whom it was vested, so quickly did he hasten to rid himself of it, as if a position that stood in the place of the laws would have been too troublesome and dangerous!

Thus it is not so much the danger of its being abused as it is that of its being degraded that makes one criticize the injudicious use of this supreme magistracy in the early days of the republic. For while it was being wasted on elections, dedications, and purely formal proceedings, there was reason to fear that it would become less formidable in time of need, and that people would become accustomed to regard as empty a title that was used exclusively in empty ceremonies.

Toward the end of the republic, the Romans, having become more circumspect, were as unreasonably sparing in their use of the dictatorship as they had formerly been lavish. It was easy to see that their fear was ill-founded; that the weakness of the capital then protected it against the

---

28. This nomination was made at night and in secret, as if it were shameful to place a man above the laws.

magistrates who were in its midst; that a dictator could, under certain circumstances, defend the public liberty without ever being able to make an attack on it; and that Rome's chains would not be forged in Rome itself, but in its armies. The weak resistance that Marius offered Sulla and Pompey offered Caesar clearly demonstrated what could be expected of internal authority in the face of external force.

This error caused them to make huge mistakes, for example, failing to name a dictator in the Catilinian affair. For since this was a question merely of the interior of the town and, at most, of some province in Italy, a dictator, with the unlimited authority that the laws gave him, would have easily quelled the conspiracy, which was stifled only by a coming together of fortuitous events, which human prudence has no right to expect.

Instead of that, the senate was content to entrust all its power to the consuls. Whence it happened that, in order to act effectively, Cicero was forced to exceed this power on a crucial point. And although the first transports of joy indicated approval of his conduct, eventually Cicero was justly called to account for the blood of citizens shed against the laws, a reproach that could not have been directed against a dictator. But the eloquence of the consul carried the day. And since even he, Roman though he was, preferred his own glory to his homeland, he sought not so much the most legitimate and safe way of saving the state as he did the way that would get him all the honor for settling this affair.[29] Thus he was justly honored as the liberator of Rome and justly punished as a lawbreaker. However brilliant his recall may have been, it undoubtedly was a pardon.

For the rest, whatever the manner in which this important commission was conferred, it is important to limit a dictatorship's duration to a very short period of time that cannot be prolonged. In the crises that call for its being established, the state is soon either destroyed or saved; and once the pressing need has passed, the dictatorship becomes tyrannical or needless. In Rome, where the dictators had terms of six months only, most of them abdicated before their terms had expired. If the term had been longer, perhaps they would have been tempted to prolong it further, as did the decemvirs with a one-year term. The dictator only had time enough to see to the need that got him elected. He did not have time to dream up other projects.

---

29. He could not have been sure of this had he proposed a dictator, since he did not dare name himself, and he could not be sure that his colleague would name him.

Chapter 7

On the Censorship

Just as the declaration of the general will takes place through the law, the declaration of the public judgment takes place through the censorship. Public opinion is the sort of law whose minister is the censor, and his task is only to apply it to particular cases, after the example of the prince.

Thus the censorial tribunal, far from being the arbiter of the people's opinion, is merely its spokesman; and as soon as it deviates from this opinion, its decisions are vain and futile.

It is useless to distinguish the mores of a nation from the objects of its esteem, for all these things derive from the same principle and are necessarily intermixed. Among all the peoples of the world, it is not nature but opinion that decides the choice of their pleasures. Reform men's opinions, and their mores will soon become purified all by themselves. Men always love what is good or what they find to be so; but it is in this judgment that they make mistakes. Hence this is the judgment whose regulation is the point at issue. Whoever judges mores judges honor, and whoever judges honor derives his law from opinion.

The opinions of a people arise from their constitution. Although the law does not regulate mores, legislation is what gives rise to them. When legislation weakens, mores degenerate; but then the judgment of the censors will not do what the force of the laws has not done.

It follows from this that the censorship can be useful for preserving mores, but never for reestablishing them. Establish censors while the laws are vigorous. Once they have lost their vigor, everything is hopeless. Nothing legitimate has any force once the laws no longer have force.

The censorship maintains mores by preventing opinions from becoming corrupt, by preserving their rectitude through wise applications, and sometimes even by making a determination on them when they are still uncertain. The use of seconds in duels, which had been carried to the point of being a craze in the kingdom of France, was abolished by the following few words of the king's edict: "As for those who are cowardly enough to call upon seconds." This judgment anticipated that of the public and suddenly fixed it. But when the same edicts tried to declare that it was also an act of cowardice to fight duels (which of course is quite true, but contrary to common opinion), the public mocked this decision; it concerned a matter about which its mind was already made up.

I have said elsewhere[30] that since public opinion is not subject to constraint, there should be no limitation placed upon the tribunal established to represent it. It is impossible to show too much admiration for the skill with which this device, entirely lost among us moderns, was put into effect among the Romans and even better among the Lacedaemonians.

When a man of bad mores put forward a good proposal in the council of Sparta, the ephors ignored it and had the same proposal put forward by a virtuous citizen. What honor for the one, what shame for the other; and without having given praise or blame to either of the two! Certain drunkards of Samos[31] defiled the tribunals of the ephors. The next day, a public edict gave the Samians permission to be filthy. A true punishment would have been less severe than impunity such as this. When Sparta made a pronouncement on what was or was not decent, Greece did not appeal its judgments.

Chapter 8

On Civil Religion[32]

At first men had no other kings but the gods, and no other government than a theocratic one. They reasoned like Caligula, and then they reasoned

---

30. I merely call attention in this chapter to what I have treated at greater length in my *Letter to d'Alembert*.
31. [Rousseau added the following in the 1782 edition: "They are from another island that the delicacy of our language prohibits me from naming at this time." The copy of the *Social Contract* that Rousseau gave to d'Ivernois has the following note: "They were from Chios and not from Samos, but given the subject matter here, I have never dared employ this word [Chios] in the text. Yet I think I am as bold as anyone; but it is not permitted to anyone to be dirty and coarse, no matter what the subject matter. The French have put so much decency into their language that one can no longer speak the truth while using it." Rousseau was afraid of a pun on the island's name.]
32. [The draft of the *Social Contract* that Rousseau sent his publisher in December 1760 did not contain this chapter. Rousseau described it in a letter of December 23, 1761 as an addition. An early draft is written on the back of the chapter on the legislator (Book II, Chapter 7), and the subject matter of the two is connected in, for example, the thinking of Machiavelli (e.g., *Discourses*, bk. 1, ch. 16). Rousseau will also have had in mind books 24–25 of the *Spirit of the Laws*. On polytheism he had

correctly. A lengthy alteration of feelings and ideas is necessary before men can be resolved to accept a fellowman as a master, in the hope that things will turn out well for having done so.

By the mere fact that God was placed at the head of every political society, it followed that there were as many gods as there were peoples. Two peoples who were alien to one another and nearly always enemies could not recognize the same master for very long. Two armies in combat with one another could not obey the same leader. Thus national divisions led to polytheism, and this in turn led to theological and civil intolerance, which are by nature the same, as will be stated later.

The fanciful notion of the Greeks that they had rediscovered their gods among the beliefs of barbarian peoples arose from another notion they had of regarding themselves as the natural sovereigns of these peoples. But in our day it is a ridiculous bit of erudition that equates the gods of different nations—as if Moloch, Saturn, and Chronos could have been the same god; as if the Phoenicians' Baal, the Greeks' Zeus, and the Romans' Jupiter could have been the same; as if there could be anything in common among chimerical beings having different names!

But if it is asked how in pagan cultures, where each state has its own cult and its own gods, there are no wars of religion, I answer that it was for this very reason that each state, having its own cult as well as its own government, did not distinguish its gods from its laws. Political war was theological as well. The territories of the gods were, so to speak, fixed by national boundaries. The gods of one people had no rights over other peoples. The gods of the pagans were not jealous gods. They divided dominion over the world among themselves. Moses himself and the Hebrew people sometimes countenanced this idea in speaking of the god of Israel. It is true they regarded as nothing the gods of the Canaanites, a proscribed people destined for destruction, and whose land they were to occupy. But note how they spoke of the divinities of neighboring peoples whom they were forbidden to attack! "Is not the possession of what belongs to your god Chamos," said Jephthah to the Ammonites, "lawfully yours? By the same right we

---

probably read Bernard le Bovier de Fontenelle's *De l'origine des fables* (1724), the article "Fable" in the *Encyclopédie* (by Louis de Jaucourt, published in 1756), and perhaps Hume's *Natural History of Religion* (1757; French translation 1759–1760). If the text is a late addition, the thinking in it was not new; it is summarized in a letter to Voltaire of August 18, 1756. The chapter immediately provoked a storm of controversy.]

possess the lands our victorious god has acquired for himself."³³ It appears to me that here was a clear recognition of the parity between the rights of Chamos and those of the god of Israel.

But when the Jews, while in subjection to the kings of Babylon and later to the kings of Syria, wanted to remain steadfast in not giving recognition to any other god but their own, their refusal, seen as rebellion against the victor, brought them the persecutions we read of in their history, and of which there is no other precedent prior to Christianity.³⁴

Since, therefore, each religion was uniquely tied to the laws of the state that prescribed it, there was no other way of converting a people except by enslaving it, nor any other missionaries than conquerors. And with the obligation to change cult being the law of the vanquished, it was necessary to begin by conquering before talking about it. Far from men fighting for the gods, it was, as it was in Homer, the gods who fought for men; each asked his own god for victory and paid for it with new altars. Before taking a fortress, the Romans summoned its gods to leave it. And when they allowed the Tarentines to keep their angry gods, it was because at that point they considered these gods to be in subjection to their own and forced to do them homage. They left the vanquished their gods, just as they left them their laws. A wreath to the Capitoline Jupiter was often the only tribute they imposed.

Finally, the Romans having spread their cult and their gods, along with their empire, and having themselves often adopted the gods of the vanquished by granting to various peoples the right of self-government,³⁵ the peoples of this vast empire gradually found themselves to have multitudes of gods and cults, which were nearly the same everywhere. And that is how paganism finally became a single, identical religion throughout the known world.

---

33. *Nonne ea quae possidet Chamos deus tuus, tibi jure debentur?* [Judges 11:24] Such is the text of the Vulgate. Father de Carrières has translated it, "Do you not believe that you have the right to possess what belongs to your god Chamos?" I do not know the force of the Hebrew text; but I see that in the Vulgate Jephthah positively acknowledges the right of the god Chamos, and that the French translator weakened this recognition by adding an "according to you," which is not in the Latin.
34. It is quite clear that the Phocian War, called the Holy War, was not a war of religion at all. Its objective was to punish sacrileges, and not to make unbelievers submit.
35. [Rousseau's term is *droit de cité*, which contemporary dictionaries define as the right to elect one's own rulers.]

Such were the circumstances under which Jesus came to establish a spiritual kingdom on earth. In separating the theological system from the political system, this made the state cease being united and caused internal divisions that have never ceased to agitate Christian peoples. But since this new idea of an otherworldly kingdom had never entered the heads of the pagans, they always regarded the Christians as true rebels who, underneath their hypocritical submission, were only waiting for the moment when they would become independent and the masters, and adroitly usurp the authority they pretended in their weakness to respect. This is the reason for the persecutions.

What the pagans feared happened. Then everything changed its appearance. The humble Christians changed their language, and soon this so-called otherworldly kingdom became, under a visible leader, the most violent despotism in this world.

However, since there has always been a prince and civil laws, this double power has given rise to a perpetual jurisdictional conflict that has made all good polity impossible in Christian states, and no one has ever been able to know whether it is the priest or the master whom one is obliged to obey.

Nevertheless, several peoples, even in Europe or nearby, have wanted to preserve or reestablish the ancient system, but without success. The spirit of Christianity has won everything. The sacred cult has always remained or again become independent of the sovereign and without any necessary link to the body of the state. Mohammed had very sound opinions. He tied his political system together very well, and as long as the form of his government subsisted under his successors, the caliphs, this government was utterly unified, and for that reason it was good. But as the Arabs became prosperous, lettered, polished, soft, and cowardly, they were subjugated by barbarians. Then the division between the two powers began again. Although it is less apparent among the Mohammedans than among the Christians, it is there all the same, especially in the sect of Ali; and there are states, such as Persia, where it never ceases to be felt.

Among us, the kings of England have established themselves as heads of the church, and the czars have done the same. But with this title, they became less its masters than its servants. They have acquired not so much the right to change it as the power to maintain it. They are not its legislators; they are merely its princes. Wherever the clergy constitutes a body,[36] it

---

36. It should be carefully noted that it is not so much the formal assemblies, such as those of France, that bind the clergy together into a body, as it is the communion of the churches. Communion and excommunication are the social compact of the

is master and legislator in its own sphere. Thus there are two powers, two sovereigns, in England and in Russia, just as there are everywhere else.

Of all the Christian writers, the philosopher Hobbes[37] is the only one who clearly saw the evil and the remedy, who dared to propose the reunification of the two heads of the eagle and the complete restoration of political unity, without which no state or government will ever be well constituted. But he should have seen that the dominating spirit of Christianity was incompatible with his system, and that the interest of the priest would always be stronger than that of the state. It is not so much what is horrible and false in his political theory as what is just and true that has caused it to be hated.[38]

I believe that if the facts of history were developed from this point of view, it would be easy to refute the opposing sentiments of Bayle and Warburton, the one holding that no religion is useful to the body politic, while the other maintains, to the contrary, that Christianity is its firmest support.[39] We could prove to the first that no state has ever been founded without religion serving as its base, and to the second that Christian law is at bottom more injurious than it is useful for the strong constitution of the state. To succeed in making myself understood, I need only give a bit more precision to the excessively vague ideas about religion that are pertinent to my subject.

---

clergy, one with which it will always be the master of the peoples and the kings. All the priests who communicate together [the text reads *communiquent*, but the sense seems to require *communient* (take communion), and one is bound to suspect a slip on the part of Rousseau or his printer] are fellow citizens, even if they should be from the opposite ends of the world. This invention is a political masterpiece. There was nothing like this among the pagan priests; thus they never made up a body of clergy.

37. [See especially Hobbes, *De Cive*, chs. 6, 17.]

38. Notice, among other texts, in Grotius' letter to his brother, dated April 11, 1643, what this learned man approves of and what he criticizes in the [Hobbes'] book *De Cive*. It is true that, prone to being indulgent, he appears to forgive the author for his good points for the sake of his bad ones. [Rousseau knew of this letter from Barbeyrac's edition of Grotius' *Law of War and Peace*. In it Grotius approves of what Hobbes says about monarchy and disapproves of what he says about religion—the opposite of Rousseau's view.] But not everyone is so merciful.

39. [Bayle, *Diverse Thoughts on the Comet* (1682); Warburton, *Divine Legation of Moses* (1737–1741), or rather, presumably, the French translation of *The Alliance between Church and State*.]

When considered in relation to society, which is either general or particular,[40] religion can also be divided into two kinds, namely, the religion of the man and that of the citizen. The first—without temples, altars, or rites and limited to the purely internal cult of the supreme God and to the eternal duties of morality—is the pure and simple religion of the Gospel, the true theism, and what can be called natural divine law.[41] The other, inscribed in a single country, gives it its gods, its own titulary patrons. It has its dogmas, its rites, its exterior cult prescribed by laws. Outside the nation that practices it, everything is infidel, alien, and barbarous to it. It extends the duties and rights of man only as far as its altars. Such were all the religions of the early peoples, to which the name of civil or positive divine law can be given.

There is a third sort of religion, which is more bizarre. In giving men two sets of legislation, two leaders, and two homelands, it subjects them to contradictory duties and prevents them from being simultaneously devout men and citizens. Such is the religion of the Lamas and of the Japanese, and such is Roman Christianity. It can be called the religion of the priest. It leads to a kind of mixed and unsociable law that has no name.

Considered from a political standpoint, these three types of religion all have their faults. The third is so evidently bad that it is a waste of time to amuse oneself by proving it. Whatever breaks up social unity is worthless. All institutions that place man in contradiction with himself are of no value.

The second is good in that it unites the divine cult with love of the laws and in that, in making the homeland the object of its citizens' admiration, it teaches them that all service to the state is service to its tutelary god. It is a kind of theocracy in which there ought to be no pontiff other than the prince and no priests other than the magistrates. To die for one's country is, then, to become a martyr; to violate its laws is to be impious; to subject a guilty man to public execration is to deliver him to the wrath of the gods: *sacer estod.*[42] However, it is bad in that, being based on error and lies, it deceives men, makes them credulous and superstitious, and drowns the true cult of the divinity in an empty ceremony. It is also bad when, on becoming exclusive and tyrannical, it makes a people bloodthirsty and intolerant, so that men breathe only murder and massacre, and believe they are performing a holy action in killing anyone who does not accept their gods. This

---

40. [The general society is the society of all human beings; the particular society is the political community.]

41. [Rousseau's most famous account of this true Christianity is to be found in "The Profession of Faith of the Savoyard Vicar," which appears within *Émile*.]

42. ["Let him be cursed."]

places such a people in a natural state of war with all others, which is quite harmful to its own security.

Thus there remains the religion of man or Christianity (not that of today, but that of the Gospel, which is completely different). Through this holy, sublime, true religion, men, in being the children of the same God, all acknowledge one another as brothers, and the society that unites them is not dissolved even at death.

But since this religion has no particular relation to the body politic, it leaves laws with only the force the laws derive from themselves, without adding any other force to them. And thus one of the great bonds of a particular society remains ineffectual. Moreover, far from attaching the hearts of the citizens to the state, it detaches them from it as from all the other earthly things. I know of nothing more contrary to the social spirit.[43]

We are told that a people of true Christians would form the most perfect society imaginable. I see but one major difficulty in this assumption, namely that a society of true Christians would no longer be a society of men.

I even say that this supposed society would not, for all its perfection, be the strongest or the most durable. By dint of being perfect, it would lack a bond of union; its destructive vice would be in its very perfection.

Each man would fulfill his duty; the people would be subject to the laws; the leaders would be just and moderate, the magistrates would be upright and incorruptible; soldiers would scorn death; there would be neither vanity nor luxury. All of this is very fine, but let us look further.

Christianity is a completely spiritual religion, concerned exclusively with things heavenly. The homeland of the Christian is not of this world. He does his duty, it is true, but he does it with a profound indifference toward the success or failure of his efforts. As long as he has nothing to reproach himself for, it matters little to him whether everything is going well or poorly down here. If the state is flourishing, he hardly dares to enjoy the public felicity, for fear of becoming puffed up with his country's glory. If the state is in decline, he blesses the hand of God that weighs heavily on his people.

For the society to be peaceful and for harmony to be maintained, every citizen without exception would have to be an equally good Christian. But if, unhappily, there is a single ambitious man, a single hypocrite, a Catiline, for example, or a Cromwell, he would quite undoubtedly gain the upper

---

43. [Later, Rousseau clarified that here he meant "contrary to the spirit of any particular society or political community," not "contrary to the spirit of the general society of all human beings."]

hand on his pious compatriots. Christian charity does not readily allow one to think ill of one's neighbors. Once he has discovered by some ruse the art of deceiving them and of laying hold of a part of the public authority, behold a man established in dignity! God wills that he be respected. Soon, behold a power! God wills that he be obeyed. Does the trustee of this power abuse it? He is the rod with which God punishes his children. It would be against one's conscience to expel the usurper. It would be necessary to disturb the public tranquility, use violence, and shed blood. All this accords ill with the meekness of a Christian. And after all, what difference does it make whether one is a free man or a serf in this vale of tears? The essential thing is getting to heaven, and resignation is but another means to that end.

What if a foreign war breaks out? The citizens march without reservation into combat; none among them dreams of deserting. They do their duty, but without passion for victory; they know how to die better than how to be victorious. What difference does it make whether they are the victors or the vanquished? Does not providence know better than they what they need? Just imagine the advantage a fierce, impetuous, and passionate enemy could draw from their stoicism! Set them face to face with those generous peoples who were devoured by an ardent love of glory and homeland. Suppose your Christian republic is face to face with Sparta or Rome. The pious Christians will be beaten, crushed, and destroyed before they realize where they are, or else they will owe their safety only to the scorn their enemies will conceive for them. To my way of thinking, the oath taken by Fabius' soldiers was a fine one. They did not swear to die or to win; they swore to return victorious. And they kept their promise. Christians would never have taken such an oath; they would have believed they were tempting God.

But I am deceiving myself in talking about a Christian republic; these terms are mutually exclusive. Christianity preaches only servitude and dependence. Its spirit is too favorable to tyranny for tyranny not to take advantage of it at all times. True Christians are made to be slaves.[44] They know it and are hardly moved by this. This brief life has too little value in their eyes.

Christian troops, we are told, are excellent. I deny this. Is someone going to show me some? For my part, I do not know of any Christian troops. Someone will mention the crusades. Without disputing the valor of the crusaders, I will point out that, far from being Christians, they were soldiers of the priest; they were citizens of the church; they were fighting for its spiritual country that the church, goodness knows how, had made temporal.

44. [Cf. Machiavelli, *Discourses*, bk 2, ch. 2.]

Properly understood, this is a throwback to paganism. Since the Gospel does not establish a national religion, no holy war is possible among Christians. Under the pagan emperors, Christian soldiers were brave. All the Christian authors affirm this, and I believe it. This was a competition for honor against the pagan troops. Once the emperors were Christians, this competition ceased. And when the cross expelled the eagle, all Roman valor disappeared.

But leaving aside political considerations, let us return to right and determine the principles that govern this important point. The right that the social compact gives the sovereign over the subjects does not, as I have said, go beyond the limits of public utility.[45] The subjects, therefore, do not have to account to the sovereign for their opinions, except to the extent that these opinions are of significance to the community. Now it is of great consequence to the state that each citizen have a religion that causes him to love his duties. But the dogmas of that religion are of no interest to either the state or its members, except to the extent that these dogmas relate to morality and to the duties that the one who professes them is required to fulfill toward others. Each man can have in addition such opinions as he pleases, without it being any of the sovereign's business to know what they are. For since the other world is outside the province of the sovereign, whatever the fate of subjects in the life to come, it is none of its business, as long as they are good citizens in this life.

There is, therefore, a purely civil profession of faith, the articles of which it belongs to the sovereign to establish, not exactly as dogmas of religion, but as sentiments of sociability, without which it is impossible to be a good citizen or a faithful subject.[46] While not having the ability to obligate anyone

---

45. "In the republic," says the Marquis d'Argenson, "each man is perfectly free with respect to what does not harm others." [D'Argenson's *Considerations on the Government of France* circulated widely in manuscript but was first published by Rey (Rousseau's publisher) in 1764, partly, one presumes, because of Rousseau's praise of it. This sentence does not appear in the published text, which is taken (as Rey admits) from a faulty manuscript. Of course, since the text was unpublished and d'Argenson had died in 1757, Rousseau was also free to play fast and loose with d'Argenson's text.] This is the invariable boundary. It cannot be expressed more precisely. I have been unable to deny myself the pleasure of occasionally citing this manuscript, even though it is unknown to the public, in order to pay homage to the memory of a famous and noteworthy man, who, even as a minister, retained the heart of a true citizen, along with just and sound opinions on the government of his country.

46. Caesar, speaking in Catiline's defense, tried to establish the dogma of the mortality of the soul. To refute him, Cato and Cicero did not waste time philosophizing. They contented themselves with showing that Caesar spoke like a bad citizen and

to believe them, the sovereign can banish from the state anyone who does not believe them. It can banish him not for being impious but for being unsociable, for being incapable of sincerely loving the laws and justice, and of sacrificing his life, if necessary, for his duty. If, after having publicly acknowledged these same dogmas, a person acts as if he does not believe them, he should be put to death; he has committed the greatest of crimes: he has lied before the laws.

The dogmas of the civil religion ought to be simple, few in number, precisely worded, without explanations or commentaries. The existence of a powerful, intelligent, beneficent divinity that foresees and provides; the life to come; the happiness of the just; the punishment of the wicked; the sanctity of the social contract and of the laws—these are the positive dogmas.[47] As for the negative dogmas, I am limiting them to just one, namely, intolerance. It is part of the cults we have excluded.

Those who distinguish between civil and theological intolerance are mistaken, in my opinion. Those two types of intolerance are inseparable. It is impossible to live in peace with those one believes to be damned. To love them would be to hate God, who punishes them. It is absolutely necessary to either reclaim them or torment them. Whenever theological intolerance is allowed, it is impossible for it not to have some civil effect;[48] and once it

---

advanced a doctrine that was injurious to the state. In fact, this was what the Roman senate had to judge, and not a question of theology.

47. [Locke in his *Letter Concerning Toleration* (1689) had similarly denied toleration to atheists, but Rousseau goes further in making the sanctity of the social contract an article of required belief.]

48. Marriage, for example, being a civil contract, has civil effects without which it is impossible for a society even to subsist. Suppose then that a clergy reaches the point where it ascribes to itself alone the right to permit this act (a right that must necessarily be usurped in every intolerant religion). In that case, is it not clear that in establishing the authority of the church in this matter, it will render ineffectual that of the prince, who will have no more subjects than those whom the clergy wishes to give him? Is it not also clear that the clergy—if master of whether to marry or not to marry people according to whether or not they accept this or that doctrine, according to whether or not they accept or reject this or that formula, according to whether they are more or less devoted to them, if it behaves prudently and holds firm—will alone dispose of inheritance, offices, the citizens, the state itself, which could not subsist if composed solely of bastards? But, it will be said, abuses will be appealed; summonses and decrees will be issued; the church's income will be seized. What rubbish! If it has a little—I will not say courage but—good sense, the clergy will let all this happen and carry on regardless. It will serenely allow the appeals, the summonses, the decrees, and the seizures, and it will end up master. It is not, it

does, the sovereign no longer is sovereign, not even over temporal affairs. Thenceforward, priests are the true masters; kings are simply their officers.

Now that there no longer is and never again can be an exclusive national religion, tolerance should be shown to all those who tolerate others, as long as their dogmas contain nothing contrary to the duties of a citizen. But whoever dares to say, "Outside the church there is no salvation" ought to be expelled from the state, unless the state is the church and the prince the pontiff. Such a dogma is good only in a theocratic government; in all other forms of government it is ruinous. The reason why Henry IV is said to have embraced the Roman religion should make every decent man, and above all any prince who knows how to reason, leave it.[49]

---

seems to me, a big sacrifice to abandon a part when one is sure of securing the whole. [Rousseau wrote a lengthy first version of this note in his draft of the *Social Contract* (Pléiade ed., 3:343–44). In it he describes the Protestants of France—who had been subjected to prolonged persecution since the revocation of the Edict of Nantes in 1685 and were forbidden to marry (since legal marriages required participation in the Catholic sacrament of the Mass) and thus, because children born out of wedlock could not inherit, unable to pass on their property to their children—as "reduced to the most horrible situation in which ever a people has found itself since the beginning of the world." It seems he then wrote a second version of the note referring to the case of the Protestant clergyman Rochette and the three brothers Grenier (on which, see David D. Bien, "Imagining the Huguenot Minority in Old Regime France," in *The Construction of Minorities*, ed. André Burguière and Raymond Grew [Ann Arbor: University of Michigan Press, 2001], 65–88, at 80–81). Then, when the four were executed in Toulouse on February 19, 1762, and when his book was in press, he substituted the present version. Finally he asked his publisher to reprint the sheet without the note, so that first editions of the *Social Contract* exist in two states, with and without the final version of the note (letters to Rey, March 11, 14, 18, and 25, 1762). Rousseau's motive in attempting to withdraw the note was evidently his fear of the reaction of the French authorities. It is worth bearing in mind that this question touched him directly: once he converted back to Protestantism in 1754 it became impossible for him to marry his companion Thérèse Levasseur; they went through a "ceremony" of marriage, which had no legal force, in 1768. Voltaire's *Treatise on Toleration*, which protested against the persecution of Protestants, was published in 1763.]

49. [Henry IV is supposed to have decided to become a Catholic because Protestant theologians acknowledged that he could be saved while being Catholic, while Catholic theologians denied that he could be saved while being Protestant. Catholicism was thus, Henry claimed, the safest bet. Thus he converted because the Catholics were more intolerant than the Protestants.]

Chapter 9

Conclusion

After laying down the true principles of political right and attempting to establish the state on this basis, it remains to support the state by means of its external relations, which would include the law of nations—commerce; the law of war and conquests; public law, leagues, negotiations, treaties, and so on.[50] But all that forms a new subject that is too vast for my nearsightedness. I should always have set my sights on things that are nearer at hand to me.

 END

---

50. [Rousseau's text has a comma after "law of nations," and commas between each item in the list; but the list that follows consists of three elements of the law of nations, so the punctuation has been revised to convey his sense.]

Index

Index

Index